The return of "an American masterpiece" (William Saroyan) long out of print.

Bill Henderson did most of his growing up in the decade of the tail-finned car, Eisenhower, rock and roll, the threat of atomic annihilation, and pervasive silence. This anguished yet loving portrait of a child of the fifties and his father reveals the secret life of that decade.

"A valediction of the 50s."—Rosellen Brown, *Chicago Tribune*

"A powerfully moving book."—Anne Tyler

"An open-hearted, funny, affecting account of family life during the silent 1950s."—*Publishers Weekly*

"Bill Henderson is akin to Tom Sawyer, to Puddinhead Wilson."—William Hogan, *San Francisco Chronicle*

His Son

A MEMOIR
BILL HENDERSON

PUSHCART PRESS
WAINSCOTT, NEW YORK

© 2000 Bill Henderson
All rights reserved
ISBN 1-888889-15-2
Published by Pushcart Press
P.O. Box 380
Wainscott, New York 11975
Distributed by
W.W. Norton & Co.

First published in hardcover by
W.W. Norton & Co.

To the memory of my father and mother,
and to families everywhere

HIS SON

March 10, 1965

H E spent the evening in the cellar at his work-bench. Now he came up the stairs and through the kitchen to the garage. She heard him rearranging the tools in the trunk of the Chevy.

"Come on, Dot," he said, returning to the kitchen.

She looked up, smiled. "After I correct these papers. You go ahead."

"Is that still on?" he nodded at the iron on the iron-ing board.

"No," she said.

But he checked the plug to make sure.

"Good night," he said, bending to kiss her on the cheek.

She noticed that it was only a little after ten—early

for him—but she didn't say anything. She just let herself be kissed.

In the bedroom, he undressed and put on his pajamas. His hand pressing against his double hernia, he went into the bathroom and came back to kneel beside the bed. He said the Lord's Prayer, and then "Now I lay me down to sleep, I pray the Lord my soul to keep. If I should die before I wake, I pray the Lord my soul to take. God bless the president of our country and help all those suffering and those in sin and show them the way to Thee. God bless Dorothy. God Bless Bill. God Bless Bob. And God bless Ruth. In His name, Amen."

He left the lamp on for her and he slept, his face turned to the light.

Later, in her own bed, my mother saw that his lips were open, parted in a different kind of way. She thought to speak to him—because it seemed to her he must be uncomfortable. But she didn't want to wake him. She turned off the light and lay back in her bed.

She heard the sound of a train on the Main Line, and then the Westminster chimes of the living-room clock. A car rushed down the road, turned at the dead end, rushed back out. In the cellar, the oil heater started.

She thought she heard something from his bed, but couldn't be certain. She heard her pulse in her ears, the rustle of the sheets against her body.

When the heater shut off, she listened again for the sound. The wind moved through the shrubbery. The clock chimed the quarter hour. The refrigerator ran, stopped. Below, the water pump labored. An early thaw had flooded a corner of the cellar.

Now she didn't dare move, because the sound of her blankets might obscure the sound she was listening for. She lay rigid, past guessing, past hope, beginning to know because she knew.

She heard a car hurry along the road, slow, turn into the driveway. It was my brother. Bob was home from the bar. She heard him open and shut the refrigerator door, she heard a knife tick against the kitchen counter.

She turned on the light.

"Bob!" she called. "Will you come here! I think something's wrong with Daddy!"

She got up, pulled a robe around her and she looked. The mouth was just the same. He could be sleeping. She touched her fingers to his cheek. "France?" she murmured. "France?"

Bob had learned artificial respiration in Boy Scouts. He tried to remember. He turned my father's body onto its back and pressed down at the base of the ribs and let up, pressed down and let up. Each time he pressed down, my father's throat gurgled. Encouraged, he continued faster, hoping he was doing at least something right. Faster and harder, thrusting my father's body deep into the mattress.

Quietly she said, "Don't bruise him, Bob."

He ran to the kitchen phone, tried to dial the family doctor, misdialed, dialed again, and was told the doctor's calls were being taken by another doctor. He woke the doctor and blurted the directions to the house. Then he ran out of the house and up the street to an intersection. When he saw car lights, he stood in the middle of the road and waved both arms.

The doctor drove carefully down the winding street. Later Bob would recall that the doctor wore a neatly arranged tie. He had taken time to dress correctly.

The doctor checked the corpse briefly and said, "I'm afraid he's gone." He scribbled a few notes on a pad, offered his sympathy, and left.

Pop's brother, Clarence, and his wife came from across town and called an undertaker they knew. The undertaker and two helpers lifted the corpse onto a pallet, covered it, and strapped it down. "I'm sorry we have to meet like this, Mrs. Henderson," the undertaker told her.

His helpers knocked off some wood and paint from the back door getting the corpse out. They swore under their breaths. They were tired and inconvenienced.

Nobody slept.

Pop's brother repeated, "They'll never be another like him. It shouldn't have happened." Unlike Pop, Clarence had faith only in Science. Science offered him no comfort.

And then, remembering Science, he asked her, "Why didn't you get him a shot of adrenalin? You should have told the doctor that."

The Turtle

On summer evenings in Ocean City, New Jersey, Pop and the family walked the boardwalk in the twilight. We stopped at the Litterer's Fresh Orange Juice Parlor for tall glasses of just-squeezed orange juice and walked back to our summer house.

Near the orange juice place was a tiny shop that sold novelties—Mexican jumping beans, miniature New Testaments, the Lord's Prayer on a penny, and, on this one night, baby soft-shelled turtles. As a nine-year-old turtle collector, I knew that the soft-shell—with protruding eyes, a long snout, and flat leathery shell—was said to be more dangerous than a snapping turtle. I bought one for fifty cents.

For two years the ugly soft-shell grew in my bed-

room aquarium while the more colorful dime-store terra-
pins around him lived a few months on dried fly turtle
food and died. The soft-shell ate anything, from tomatoes
to dog food, with a hearty viciousness and thrived. I
thought he was immortal.

One night I put the soft-shell in the bathroom sink
while I soaked his aquarium in suds. I ate my dinner and
afterward found that a slow drip from the hot-water tap
had scalded the turtle to death.

I carried his body to Pop. Pop rushed the turtle to his
basement workshop and attached him to a small generator he had built—the front foot to one wire, the back to
another.

I whirled the handle of the generator as he instructed
and the turtle twitched. "Faster," Pop ordered.

I cranked furiously and the soft-shell shivered. We
both hoped that it was the reviving turtle and not just the
jolts of electricity that caused the shivers. I cranked until
both arms were sore, and then Pop cranked.

But when we detached the turtle from the generator
he was still.

Pop had done all he knew how.

It was the first time we had met death together.

Rome

THE guidebook said the catacombs were just outside the walls of Rome, right down the Appian Way. The walk would be important, I thought, a chance to imagine the life of the early Christians.

The guidebook didn't say that the catacombs were miles from Rome and that the Appian Way was now a busy highway without sidewalks.

At the catacombs, a group of tourists had assembled. We waited until a cranky priest escorted us underground. Here the first Christians had held ceremonies and hidden. I saw bones and artifacts and then climbed into the spring day.

Thousands of miles away my father said his prayers and died.

17

The next morning a telegram had arrived for me at the American Express office. "Call home collect immediately. Urgent. Mother."

She said on the phone, "Bill, Daddy's died."

She told me how it happened. She was worried about me all alone. I asked when the funeral was and said I would change my boat ticket for an airline ticket and be there.

I wandered around unknown blocks, up the Spanish Steps to Trinti del Monti and down, and then, a half hour later in the middle of an intersection my first reaction. I laughed.

If Pop had been with me I would have slapped him on the back in congratulation. "You did it, Pop," I said outloud. "You got out of it just the way you wanted. No pain. No fuss."

I laughed at myself. I was ridiculous for ever doubting him. His life had been consistent to the end. His God had not failed him.

I entered a small Catholic church and sat in a pew surrounded by old women in black with bowed heads. Tourists prowled the statues. Giggling school girls dropped their book bags and knelt in a chapel at the side. I bowed my head but couldn't pray. I thought it was because of the statues.

I left the church and searched for another without statues, but I was in the wrong town.

I decided to go back to my hotel to pray. On the way I passed a church that announced itself on a sign outside as "Scotch-Episcopal." A custodian unlocked the door for me, thinking I was a tourist who would soon leave. I sat in the middle of the empty church and looked at the undecorated walls and the simple pulpit. No statues. This was Pop's church.

But I couldn't pray. I opened a Bible from the pew rack and asked God to pick a page with revelations about Pop's death. I shut the Bible and opened it and read a page, and shut it and opened it again, but none of the passages offered a message.

On the back of the telegram I started a eulogy for Pop. I would salute him at his funeral.

"My father was not the simple man he appeared to be," I wrote, "but he was not a man of words. So he came to the church, to the evangelists, and he let their words speak for him. In the hymns of the church and the seemingly banal language of the ministers, my father's soul found its expression . . ."

The custodian behind me was moving around and coughing.

I tried again to pray but I didn't know who to pray to. Finally I asked Pop to pray for me.

Two blocks away a sign outside a Catholic church advertised "lessons in English for non-Catholics." Two priests with an altar boy were preparing their vestments. I approached one of them. "Father, could I talk to you?"

He nodded with a question in his eyes, since Mass was about to begin.

"My father just died in the United States and I wondered if you could say a prayer for him?"

"Oh, I'm awfully sorry. This is our priest in charge here," he said, indicating the other man. "Father, his father has just died in the States."

"I'm terribly sorry," the other priest said.

"I wondered if you would say a prayer for him."

"Certainly." He paused. "Was he a Catholic?"

"No."

"I see . . . well, are you a Catholic?"

"No, I was brought up a Presbyterian."

"I see . . . I'd be glad to say a prayer for him, of course."

I bought a Bible for Mother. I thought this gift would comfort her in the hope that I still believed as she did.

On the plane back I drank bourbon and cried a little and imagined that Pop was up here among the white clouds in some sort of Hallmark card heaven.

In just ten days I would have seen Pop again. The boat would have left Naples two days after he died.

Pop knew my plans. He could have waited for me, I thought.

It was almost as if he had died on purpose when he did, politely leaving me time to get to the funeral. But pointedly not waiting to see me again.

Ceremonies

MOTHER and I sat at the kitchen table in Bryn Mawr and she told me about Pop's last night. With a Kleenex tucked in her dress pocket, she would tell the story over and over in the next few days.

Bob and I went to the barbershop to have my hair cut for the funeral.

It would be our first funeral. We didn't miss Pop as much as we imagined was appropriate. His death had become an embarrassment.

I remembered when Pop had asked Bob and me to help him trim the dead wood from the backyard trees. Dead wood only. Pop always refused to prune live wood because that would cause the trees to suffer. We protested that we had better things to do. But Pop insisted and produced his homemade pruning tool—a pair of clippers bolted to the end of a long pole and operated with a length of rope. It didn't work very well, and, bragging of my teenage strength, I said that I'd scramble up the trees and pluck out the dead limbs with my bare hands. But Pop kept poking at the trees, and we began to laugh at him, his two sons together. We left him in the yard alone. We walked away, laughing.

Bob and I left the barbershop and went home to dinner. Pop's chair sat empty at the end of the table. There were no other seats and I was still standing. Pop had sat in this chair since he was married. It was his, not mine.

But something was expected of me. A ceremony? I sat down. "Is this where I sit now?" I attempted with a tight smile. An aunt glared at me. It had been a ceremony after all.

I lay on the den floor in front of the television set and watched for hours. I fell asleep and later woke to a dark house. I noticed that Mom's bedroom door was still open a crack as it always had been when we were children.

Whenever I woke I switched on the TV in order to sleep again. In the morning I watched children's cartoon shows. Others found comfort where they could.

Mom would tell her story of Pop's death. The guests would chatter about their children, grandchildren, and pets, and leave.

A typical sympathy card suggested "whatever

thoughts sustain you in these moments I hope are with you."

"Wouldn't it be nice to imagine that Francis is with my mother now in heaven?" smiled twice-divorced Cousin Betty, the family scandal.

All the neighbors, friends, and relatives brought cakes, pies, and flowers. The house was filled with people eating and the scent of blossoms.

Nobody cried.

I drove the family to the church and we waited in a side room until the congregation had been seated in the chapel.

The minister arrived and took Mom's hand and said he was very sorry and shook hands with Bob, Ruth, and me before leaving for the altar.

As the door to the chapel closed behind him I noticed individuals sitting in the back by themselves, perhaps people Pop had worked with during his thirty-seven years at General Electric. Pop would have been abashed by their coming to honor him. He would have lowered his head and said "Aw."

He had been honored before, by the officials of the General Electric Company. They gave him a dinner, made speeches, handed him an inscribed wood and plastic plaque. Pop shoved the plaque in his bureau drawer under some underwear. Mom dug it out and hung it on the den wall. "For a quarter century of service to the company," it said over the signatures of Pop's boss and the president of GE.

I refused to view Pop's body and so did Bob and Ruth. To me it was just a body now.

But Mother went to say goodbye and covered him with a silk cloth. "I covered my father and mother and I will cover Daddy," she said.

When the casket was closed we assembled in the front pew. Behind us, Cousin Betty cried, "Francis, my baby. Francis."

The minister said a prayer. We sang a hymn. He said another prayer and read from Psalms. We left the casket for the undertaker's men, and lined up the cars for the trip to the cemetery.

At the cemetery, there were several funerals, at several striped tents. Pop's tent was green and white, and open on three sides.

We huddled next to the casket holding arms. I was determined that I wouldn't be the first to weep. I decided not to read my eulogy. This was Pop's funeral, his show not mine, and I would keep my mouth shut.

The minister seemed in a hurry. After a short prayer, he read from Ecclesiastes. I knew the passage almost by heart. We had read it in high-school ceremonies because it was non-denominational, acceptable to Catholics, Jews, Protestants, and teenage atheists. "For everything there is a season, and a time for every matter under heaven: a time to be born, and a time to die . . . "

We left the coffin sitting on the electric jack and returned to the car.

I had let them bury Pop in a stock ceremony, like he was a stock character.

Nothing had been said of my Pop's renegade ideas like heaven and hell, and eternal life and the real Second Coming of Jesus. Unlike these Main Line Christians, he never doubted or equivocated. But we got rid of him, all of us, as if he were ordinary.

Back at the house, it was time to eat again. The mourners jammed the den and I couldn't get to the TV.

The tears slammed into me so hard and so suddenly that I didn't have time to escape. I hadn't cried for years, and didn't know what this was.

I ran upstairs, frantically looking for a hiding place. In the attic I sat on a rolled-up rug. "You know it all now, Pop. I thought I'd be such a hot shot telling you about Europe. But now you know it all. All there is to know."

My tears were a child's tears because his death had made me his child again.

Weeks later the crocuses were up and the willow leaves were starting. Mom and I talked in the back yard.

"I'm surprised there wasn't at least some joy for Pop's going to heaven," I said. "You all say you are Christians and we will see each other again, but nobody at the funeral mentioned that."

She nodded. "Daddy's in heaven. I think of all the

beautiful sights he's seeing now—even more beautiful than these flowers. But I'm alone and that's why I'm sad. I have to live on earth and fill out the tax forms and take care of the car, and do all the things by myself that we used to do together. Daddy's happy. I shouldn't be sad. I guess I'm just selfish."

Fishing

By noon, three-hundred-fifty-pound Luke was already drunk. He sat on a stool and yelled at the college kids at the other end of the bar. "This is my country and I love her!" He turned to the United Parcel Service driver drinking shots and beers next to him. "I fought for her! I almost gave her my life! Now they're trying to kill her!"

The two college kids, short-haired Villanova law students, were having fun: "Sure, Luke. If we don't bomb the North, the whole Vietnamese navy is going to sail in and shell California!" they laughed.

Luke couldn't attack them. So he started to cry. Which delighted the kids.

It was too noisy where I was. So I moved Pop's letters and my notebook to another table around the

27

corner in the L-shaped tavern. The regulars accepted my presence in the place. I was another student to them, one of the okay types—a hard worker, polite.

That morning the *Philadelphia Inquirer* had predicted war with China. The editorial mentioned "megadeaths." That's how deaths would be measured in an atomic war. More anonymous deaths, just like Pop's. I was determined that the draft board would not make me into a megadeath in Asia.

I wanted to find out who my father had been and then be sure who I was, and then write one good true book. And then kill myself to prove I had been brave all along and wasn't trying to draft dodge just to save my own skin. I tacked that suicide pledge to my apartment wall.

My draft board defenses were many. I was enrolled in divinity school. And just in case that didn't work I was also trying to trick a girl into pregnancy by promising *coitus interruptus* but interrupting a few seconds too late. And if marriage and a child didn't keep me out of the army, there was always the psychiatrist who had once certified to the draft board that I was an alcoholic.

At that point I had given up any hope of becoming president of the United States. My alcoholism would be on my permanent record and no ex-drunk would ever make it to the presidency. It was a large option I had cancelled. But I had to survive this war so that I could write about my father.

That's why I had been stealing his letters, a few at a

time, from Mom's bureau drawer. She probably would have given them to me, but I couldn't have risked her refusal. I'd go to the tavern, copy the letters into a notebook, and then sneak them back to where I'd gotten them. They were love letters my mother and father had written to each other from 1935 to 1938, the years before they were married.

Years earlier from college I had written to Pop: "I have lived all eighteen years of my life with you and I don't know anything about your past, your parents, your grandparents. Nothing. Please write back and tell me about your life."

No answer.

That summer Pop and I went fishing, the two of us alone in Ocean City's Great Egg Harbor Bay. With the rented rowboat anchored a mile from shore, he had no easy escape.

"Pop, I don't know anything about you," I began, dangling my feet in the water and holding the fishing pole for the fish that never bit that afternoon.

"There's nothing to know."

"Well, at least tell me where you grew up."

"In Audubon, New Jersey."

"What was it like?"

"We had a house near the Delaware."

"What else?"

"There was a lighted buoy on the river that I saw from my bedroom window. It flashed on and off every night. There isn't too much else. Once some kids broke a window in a neighbor's house and I got blamed."

"How long did you live in Audubon?"

"Just when I was young. Then my dad got a better job with Swift and Company and we moved to Philadelphia, to Fifty-second and Pine."

I waited, and fished.

"My brothers and I used to help dad load the Swift meat wagon at four in the morning and sometimes we'd go around with him and the company horse and I'd help him make deliveries to the butcher shops. He did a good job and they wanted to make him sales manager for all of South Jersey, but he didn't want it. He retired early."

"What kind of a guy was Grandpop then?"

Pop stopped and stared at the water. He pressed his lips together. "He drank."

Pop stopped and I waited.

"He used to crawl across the park at night on his hands and knees. Once my mother had to lock him in the closet for a day until he sobered up. Uncle Clarence and Uncle Jim grabbed him and dragged him upstairs and helped her shove him in the closet and she locked it. He begged to be let out but she wouldn't let him out."

Pop stared. "It was awful."

I didn't say anything.

"One day outside the house he came up the street drunk. I was with my mother and he grabbed her. I hit him."

"How?"

"Twice. In the stomach."

His lips worked but he didn't speak, trying to control his tears. "I ran away from home. I stayed with a neighbor around the block for two weeks. I didn't tell them where I was."

There was nothing more he wanted to say. He fished for the rest of the afternoon in silence. To Pop that had been everything, hitting his father.

But I couldn't dismiss his life so easily.

Maybe it was hidden in the house. I had to move fast. The relatives and mother would soon clean out his drawers and closet, give away his clothes to Goodwill and throw away other stuff that seemed of no value. Uncle Clarence had already appraised his tools in the basement workshop.

Every item he left behind might reveal him. I determined to catalogue it all.

The house was a museum of his handmade creations: bookcases, a desk, a record player, a wooden wagon with 1945 automobile tags (a Christmas gift for Bob and me), a radio, and a snow blower that he fashioned out of a nonfunctioning tree sprayer—the snow blower didn't work either, shooting snow straight up into the air to fall back on Pop, the amused operator.

His engineering textbooks were stored in the den in a glass-door cabinet. I investigated them for marginal scribbles, doodles, dog ears, anything that would suggest the student Pop. But the books were clean, not even an underline. No frustrated rips, tears, or exclamations. The titles intimidated me—*Elements of Heat Power Engi-*

*neering; Lightning Arrester Grounding by Interconnec-
tion,* and *Engineering of Power Plants.*

In his bedroom drawers were Pennsylvania automobile registrations for Chevrolets bought in 1942, 1948,
and 1961 and Pontiacs in 1952 and 1957, plus driver's
licenses, draft cards (he was slightly too young for the
First World War and just over forty for the Second),
worn-out wallets, tie clips, cufflinks, a box of pennies,
Canadian coins, work orders ("Frank please visit cus-
tomer . . . "), job reports in his precise handwriting.

I found a program he had saved from my high-
school graduation and a hand-crafted Valentine's Day
card from me dated February 13, 1951—"Have a nice
Valentine's Day, you hear!" I threatened under my draw-
ing of a juvenile deliquent with a cigarette in his mouth
and a knife in hand. It was signed "Love, Bill" with a
flourish.

From his college days was a notebook of important
addresses (including those of two women) and dates
(such as his father's wedding, August 11, 1898, and the
day Pop joined Bethany Temple Church in Philadelphia,
November 1, 1925) and cash records (Pop paid $162.50
tuition in 1923 at the University of Pennsylvania).

Under the notebook were documents of membership in the Canto, North Carolina, and the Easton, Pennsylvania, YMCAs; a certificate of baptism for his mother
dated 1892; a short letter from his mother enclosing a
booklet titled *Salvation: The Eternal Question* and sealed
with "Go To Church on Sunday" stickers; a wartime

identification card for his father issued by the captain of the port of Sarasota, Florida, in 1943; an invitation to a fraternity dance in 1925 in the form of a fake legal summons; and a blue box holding a silver medal dated June 23, 1919 and presented to Pop by the First School District of Pennsylvania: "The Issac A. Sheppard Medal for Worth and Diligence."

There was a Bible with an undated inscription to him from Mom and various booklets—the bylaws of his Masonic Lodge; a booklet about how Christian Science was the true way, and another by a fundamentalist sect about the fatal error of Christian Science; a pocket-sized version of Proverbs and of Luke and several of John including one printed by Jane E. Ely, Garden City, Kansas: *The It Is Finished Work of The Lamb Slain From The Foundation of the World According To the Gospel of John.*

An undated program from a Moral Rearmament dinner meeting listed the songs for the evening and suggested that "you give God ten minutes every day and you'll find convictions in your mind. They are God's directions for you. Write them down."

A postcard from Oil City, Pennsylvania, dated March 26, 1935 said, "Dear Friend, It has taken some time but the Lord led a young man to me tonight. How are you doing. A. M. Turney."

An English class assignment in a notebook for Electrical Engineering, University of Pennsylvania Class of 1924, was: "Who I am and Why I'm Here." Pop had added mysteriously, "Who I am/John I Will."

Was he supposed to write the paper under that pseudonym? Was his "John I Will" an indication of rebellion at the topic? The paper he wrote was nowhere in the drawers.

Seemingly torn from his notebook, the same one with the "Who I Am" assignment were the following instructions to himself, undated:

"Do not procrastinate, tell others."

"By your own life show others."

"Have fellowship with whomever you meet and witness the love of God which passes understanding."

"Be not ashamed of God in any sense for He is my life and in Him I have my being."

It wasn't much but I had found something: it had not always been easy for him to witness the Word.

He had been ashamed.

Letters

AFTER the funeral I asked Mom to draw me a family tree. From memory she traced her own family to 1700, recalling dozens of families and all their children, but she knew little about Pop's family. He had told her almost nothing.

She said there had been Shillers and Petersens on his side and we both remembered a story Grandpop Henderson had told about his grandfather who served for the North in the Civil War, was shot, and saved by a buddy who hauled him out of a stream and nursed his wounds.

The rest was silence.

At the bar I hid the letters on the seat beside me, and behind a pile of books. I worked at copying them one by one.

The first, dated September 22, 1931, was a short thank-you note from my mother. Pop had driven her from her parents' home in Philadelphia to her new teaching job in Westfield, New Jersey. She called him "Frank," and suggested that he might telephone her, and then she thanked him and signed the note "Sincerely, Dorothy." After that there was nothing for six years, except for Christmas cards from Mom to Pop in 1934 and 1936, signed formally.

In January of 1937, when Pop was thirty-six, he wrote from Philadelphia to Westfield, "Letters are out of my line and besides are dangerous." Later in the month, he wrote, "I don't know how to use those sugar-coated words. They're a new language to me which you'll have to teach me . . . "

A few days later he said, "I know that your pupils can't help but like a teacher who balls them out and at the same time tells them with her eyes she doesn't mean it." He said he had escaped an unwanted job-assignment in Norfolk, Virginia: "We don't usually appreciate the common things well, like being home, etc. until we leave them . . . Maybe I'd make a philosopher or something."

A week later he wrote, "I'm glad you had a good time over the weekend. I did too. I guess I was disappointing in some things but anyway we had a good time, didn't we."

On April 6, 1937, he wrote from Philadelphia to Westfield: "I went down to the Navy Yard yesterday to see how they're getting along on one of the new cruisers there. Everything was fine and dandy so I left . . . I went over to the church last night thinking there would be a minstrel rehearsal. I was fooled as it was postponed until tonight. Anyway a few of the fellows were there counting money including Harry. After we were through we had a bowling match at Colonial Rec. Did you ever go in for that sport, Dot? We were terrible. I think the highest score was 128." He enclosed a cartoon cut from a newspaper of a Negro who had caught a bird. A white man with an explorer's hat was upset. He had ordered the Negro to catch a butterfly. Pop didn't refer to the cartoon in his letter.

On June 3, 1937, he wrote to her in Westfield: "I was over to the church tonight to look the blower over. At the trustees' meeting last night it was mentioned it could not be used because it was too noisy. After a little work on it there was hardly any noise to speak of except the windage of the fan. They were having choir practice at the time but it seems to be just enough sound to throw the choir off key."

On November 8, 1937, he wrote to Westfield: "There is something going on at the church tonight. There are about 200 women. My mother came in saying that more ginger cakes were needed so would I take her to Fifty-third and Girard Ave. where there were a few left. So I did and we saved the day or something."

In an undated letter, he wrote: "Glad to hear you are a good Methodist and went to church Sunday. You're pretty good to remember the text. I suppose you think I

37

am a nut on religion but honestly I'm not. I like to learn of the deeper things in life, and you can really find enjoyment in them too." He enclosed a book, *I Was a Pagan* "about the Oxford Movement. Although I'm not identified with the movement I'm interested in it, as I probably told you." As he often did, he closed the letter: "So I'll say goodnight Dottie and don't forget to be good and do good."

In an undated letter with a smudged December 1937 postmark, he explained: "You know I sometimes blow hot and cold on different things. I wish it were not so. I believe that is because of a selfish attitude and it is only by consecrating our lives to God's will that we can go forward. Knowing and asking that He will not allow anything to come to pass that is not according to His Divine Plan for us. Knowing also He will thoroughly furnish us for any good work . . . "

That fall they had become engaged and planned a quick wedding, a plan which they later changed to June, 1938, for unexplained reasons. As their marriage approached, Pop often sent Mom newspaper clippings, such as one headlined: "Spiritual Bond Held Family Aid" and another: "Answers to Ten Questions Show Chances for Marital Bliss."

On January 8, 1938, he wrote, "I haven't found a date tonight and it seems sort of lonely. It looks like you spoiled me. But it has been more or less a habit to do nothing and as Greta Garbo says 'I want to be alone.' "

Four days later he wrote, "Hoping perchance I'll get

out of the fog that gets me sometime . . . "

What fog? I wondered at the bar, frustrated by his vagueness. Depression? Loss of faith?

He had said letter-writing was dangerous. Had he known his child would come looking for him in these letters?

In another letter sent the same week, Pop said, "I went over to Pete's home in Chester Monday night . . . One of the fellows could sing and he did his best to entertain the crowd. Most of the time was spent in drinking beer. They had a beer keg down there and everybody was kept in supply of fresh beer. Also sandwiches were being passed incessantly. I didn't take any beer but Pete had plenty of ginger ale on hand too, so I just sat back and took it all in. That's the first beer party I was ever to and to tell you the truth there wasn't much life to it outside of a little house fly. How much more fun you can have with the silly little games we have, I think. I prefer that to either beer parties or bridge parties. Nobody is bored."

On January 28, 1938: "Here it is Saturday night and way up in the mountains . . . checking for a leak in a nitrogen gas tank but it is so cold that the soapy water I use freezes like the frosting on one of your cakes." A week later he said that he might have to go to Jacksonville, Florida, for three months. The National Container Corporation was putting up a papermill and GE wanted "someone to take over the electrical end of it."

From the Commodore Hotel in Washington, D.C.,

39

he wrote on February 14, 1938: "Then last Saturday night I thought I'd see *Snow White and the Seven Dwarfs* by Walt Disney. There's a picture for you. You almost forget they are colored drawings there is so much life and character in them . . . I wouldn't advise it for small children though, as there are parts in it that are weird and terrifying. Other parts are nice as you'd want them to be. Anyway, it takes your interest from start to finish. A woman had a small boy next to me and he became scared at different parts. He actually got up and hid behind the seat so he wouldn't see it."

On April 7, 1938 he said: "Above all, Dot, I think we should consider our plans in relationship to God and how we can come into a closer fellowship with Him. I lose sight of this fact sometimes to my sorrow. It's always flesh against the spirit. I hope you understand and again you are so swell about everything."

On May 13, 1938—the month before their marriage —he wrote from Philadelphia to Westfield about a sermon preached on the coronation of the king of England: "Everything in the coronation was done in the name of Jesus Christ and how we neglect that in our own country to our detriment. The Christian Life is the only life, Dottie, and I hope you are making progress along those lines. It's more than you can put into words to explain it, as you probably know by experience."

In an undated, unaddressed letter at this place in the stack, he said, "Once in a while I've been able to keep my thoughts on my work and am able to see the light. But that same feeling persists, Dottie. I hate to say it but I must be frank for our own happiness. I love you, Dottie, and you're the only comforting one I know."

On May 26, 1938, from the Commodore Hotel in Washington, D.C., to Westfield via air mail he wrote in the last letter before their marriage: "I feel as one who has condemned that which he has allowed. I do so much with all my heart want to do that which is right and only through God's grace will I be able to do so. I can't do it in my own strength as I have been trying to do so far and yet haven't found relief. I certainly have to surrender something if we are to be happy together. I hope we can get a chance to really pray it out together at the house. I believe we have so far only scratched the surface. If we are truly surrendered to God's will we shall surely find the answer and the blessed assurance in our hearts. I'm sorry to have left things slide so far, hoping against hope or something that we were going along in the right way. Maybe it is a lesson we must learn so that we may help others to find their answer. Anyway, Dot, what really matters now is our relationship between God and ourselves."

There was no clue anywhere in the letters about the cause of his anxiety except for a letter from Mom to him on February 23, 1938. Typically, she wrote in the evening while listening to the radio. Her favorite program was "The Carnation Milk Hour." That night they were playing Victor Herbert's best-known compositions in honor of Herbert's birthday. She was cheerful and encouraging.

Mother reported that Luke 20, verses 35–36 may indeed say "But they which shall be accounted worthy to obtain that world and the resurrection from the dead neither marry nor are given in marriage," but she had visited her minister and he said that Mark didn't agree with Luke on marriage. She cited Mark 20, verses 6 to 8: "But from the beginning of creation God made them male and female. For this reason a man shall leave his father and mother and be joined to his wife and the two shall become one flesh. So they are no longer two but one flesh."

Mom's final letter consoled him: "Remember him always, France. He can and will show you the way to rid your heart and mind of those worrisome ideas and habits that beset you so constantly."

She had been out to see their first house at 124 Crosshill Road, Penn Wynne, and reported: " . . . how the sun streams in those many windows, making it all so bright and cheery! If you were there we'd probably have been chasing up and down to see how the sun shines in the dining room and then the bedrooms!"

Two years, ten months, and twenty days after their marriage, I was born, the first of three children.

I packed up the last of the letters and slipped them back in Mom's drawer. His letters made no sense. This was a man who was not yet my father.

I'd have to search for Pop in memories.

42

Days

SOME mornings Pop's chalk drawings waited for the children on the kitchen blackboard. He had worked on them into the night. My favorites were his barnyard with pigs, chickens, and cows; or his fishing wharf with sailboats under full sail, and gulls and billowing clouds. I marveled at what Pop knew and demonstrated to us in those drawings.

At breakfast, Mom squeezed oranges for fresh juice, dosed us with cod liver oil (she remembered the foul odor of the oil,) mixed the Ovaltine and cooked hot cereal. Pop, the chalk artist, sitting between Ruth in her highchair and me, spooned his cereal and listened to Reverend Carl McIntire's "Twentieth Century Reformation Hour" on the radio. Reverend McIntire shouted that the Communists were advancing across Europe and the Russians would soon have the A-bomb and that meant the End was near just as predicted in Revelation : "Behold I am coming soon, bringing my recompense, to repay every one for what he has done. I am the Alpha and the Omega, the first and the last, the beginning and the end. Blessed are those who wash their robes, that they may have the right to the tree of life and that they may enter the city by the gates. Outside are the dogs and sorcerers and fornicators and murderers and idolaters, and every one who loves and practices falsehood."

Reverend McIntire's words—even the few I understood—didn't scare me, and neither did his sadistic frenzy. My Pop knew Reverend McIntire's God and what that God required of us, just as Pop understood the details of barnyards and wharves. He loved us and wouldn't lie to us. Pop and God would see that we were on the right side in the coming terror. The rule for kids was Be Good. Pop and God would take care of the rest.

Mother, who liked just about everybody—and was liked in return—treated everybody as if they were good: the Degger's Dairy milkman, the Freihoffer's bread man, the teachers, the minister, most of the neighbors. Pop, in his short breakfast grace, murmured under Reverend McIntire's shrieks, would often include Harry Truman in his list of good, Godfearing men.

Reverend McIntire raged through the breakfasts of my childhood. Everywhere I saw evidence of the End he predicted. For example, Uncle Chic appeared one day in a sailor's uniform and didn't return for three years; the government warned us that enemy subs lurked off the coast and we had to put up black shades on the summer house windows to block the light and confuse attackers; I picked up a newspaper from the front steps and ran inside shouting the headline to prove I could read such profundities: "War In Korea!"

One bright summer day, Mom and we children were walking the boardwalk when a navy propeller fighter roared in from the sea, U-turned, and crashed suddenly just beyond the breakers. The pilot climbed from his cockpit and stood on the wing until lifeguards rowed out and rescued him.

"Why did the plane crash?" I asked Mother later. She said she didn't know and I was baffled and scared. There had to be a reason for everything, didn't there? She said she didn't know the reason.

Sin of some sort caused the plane crash, I figured. That's what Pop might have said, but he was away at work for two weeks.

To Pop, sin was real. Sin was the reason for everything terrible. Heaven and hell were actual places. Jesus and God were people who lived with us, not just pleasant suburban abstractions. The events of the world and of our every day were crammed with meaning and grand purpose.

Pop did not speak directly about such matters. He let Reverend McIntire do that.

When my instructor, McIntire, complained as he

often did that he was too poor, that the devil was at the door and he couldn't possibly continue his radio ministry unless all his listeners rushed him money, I wrote: "Dear Dr. McIntire, my name is Billy and I am in bed with measles. I like your program. Here is twenty-five cents. This is my allowance for the week. I will send you another twenty-five cents next week."

Reverend McIntire read my letter on the air and declared that it was most touching to get that kind of contribution from a bedridden child and wouldn't God be pleased if everybody sacrificed like that. He mailed me a purple plastic spoon "to feed the gospel to the world" and a small red velvet wall plaque that told me in gold letters "I can do all things through Christ which strengthenest me. John 3: 20."

"All things!" I wondered. I could do "all things" as long as I pleased Jesus by cleaning up my room, memorizing my Sunday School Bible verses, getting good report cards, and not picking my nose.

In Penn Wynne elementary school I learned about the Permanent Record. This record was similar to God's heavenly record and to the less important records of Santa Claus and Peter Rabbit.

The Permanent Record was kept by Mrs. Morris, the principal, and would be on file on earth forever. When somebody crayoned "Minnie Morris" on the school wall

—meant as an unflattering comparison of our principal to Minnie Mouse—we were warned that the insulting child had to confess to Mrs. Morris or the crime would be entered on the Permanent Record of every child.

Nobody confessed.

Our moral supervisor in kindergarten was Mrs. Hotchkiss. She assured the class that if we didn't quiet down the crack in the ceiling would widen and the entire ceiling would plunge down on us. We could see the crack growing every day, couldn't we, just look up there.

If the crack didn't work, she threatened us with the Stuff, a mysterious substance stored in a brown jar on the top shelf of the closet. Mrs. Hotchkiss said that the Stuff, when smeared on a child's lips, would glue the mouth shut for three days. That meant you couldn't eat, talk, or drink water. The Stuff meant death.

Evil to Mrs. Hotchkiss was Chucky Charles. She knew awful things about Chucky that none of us knew and she was constantly ordering Chucky to sit in the dark immense hall by himself for mysterious crimes.

We were weaving potholders one day, when suddenly a shrieking Chucky was being dragged across the room toward the Stuff. Chucky wet his pants and the class cried with him "No, no, no, Mrs. Hotchkiss!"

She reached up to the shelf and held the brown bottle in Chucky's face. She looked at us for a while, stared down at the writhing Chucky, and slowly untwisted the top. When we were all screaming loud enough to bring down the ceiling, she smiled and put the Stuff back on the shelf.

Something changed for me that day.

Mrs. Hotchkiss had tortured us. But she was the teacher, the good person. I suspected she was just as evil as she said Chucky was. And I didn't understand that.

In third grade, the class watched tadpoles change into frogs. Most of the tadpoles had four legs and were just beginning to lose their tails, when Barry Lurton—a kid with the habit of grinning and simultaneously touching his tongue to the point of his nose—heaved the aquarium out of the second-floor window.

As we stood around the broken glass and almost-frog bodies, our third-grade teacher tried to console us. "It wasn't Barry's fault," she said.

Wasn't Barry's fault? I wondered. Then whose fault was it?

Sure Barry was retarded, but it was still his fault. Otherwise the deaths must be God's fault because God made Barry the way he was.

But that was unthinkable.

Barry went to special school the next week and I tried to forget about it.

In sixth grade, Mr. Fritz made us memorize all of Kipling's poem "If".

If you can force your heart and nerve and sinew
To serve your turn long after they are gone
And so hold on when there is nothing in you

Except the Will which says to them: "Hold on" . . .
Yours is the Earth and everything that's in it
And—which is more—
You'll be a Man, my son.

It sounded like what Pop might have said. But soon it seemed more complicated, this being a Man. I walked the halls with my shoulders hunched up. That's the way football players walked. I didn't know about their shoulder pads.

Pop and Carl McIntire were silent about sex. But in the library the boys clustered around *Popular Mechanics* and giggled at the "RUPTURED?" ads for hernia supports. Was the truss a sexual device?

At a class picnic Sammy Mack stuck a hot dog in his fly and wiggled it in front of girls. In the halls Dirty Dee Bond was "giving the finger"—whatever that meant. I went to a spin-the-bottle party and kissed a girl named Alice Wilbert.

Alice told the other girls that she liked me and I courageously walked her home from school. At her door she began to cry. "What's wrong, Alice?" I asked. But she only cried harder.

The next day, playing first base, I dropped a foul ball in my eye and she screeched with laughter as I lay twisting in the dust. "What an ass!" she hollered.

A girl said "ass." And I had no idea why.

That spring we studied the mating habits of the Praying

49

Mantis. Mr. Fritz instructed us to watch while the female Mantis was serviced by the male. The boys gasped as she then turned and bit his head off.

Rumors on the playground were about "doing it" and what a girl was like down there and taking off your clothes to "do it."

I resolved never to take off my clothes with a girl. Ever.

Penn Wynne elementary school expected us to learn the adult graces in an extracurricular dance class.

Pop, in one of his rare direct orders—later overruled by Mom in one of her rare direct confrontations—said "no dancing class."

Evenings

WHEN I was sick, Pop rushed upstairs after arriving home from work. He knelt by my bed, his hand on my fevered forehead, praying aloud to God for my recovery. Sometimes I was happy enough to be sick and missing school. I was embarrassed by his passion. Mom's doctors and prescriptions were fast enough for me.

When I was well I played the evenings away with the neighborhood kids outside. Pop called me in for dinner with his two-fingered, two-note whistle, which was unlike the plastic whistles, hohoos, and bells of other parents. Often he had brought home small gifts from work for each of us, and handed them to us as we kissed his scratchy whiskers.

I remember especially a metal globe. My father handed me the world.

Before dinner—served without fail at six P.M.—either Mom or Pop said grace. After dinner, each of us recited a Bible verse. "Jesus wept," I said if lazy. "Wine is a mocker, strong drink is raging and whoever is deceived thereby is not wise," I'd recite if I wanted to make Pop proud of me.

Then one of the children read a two-paragraph lesson from the *Upper Room,* a Presbyterian magazine that also told us what Bible section to read outloud that evening. Mom or Pop finished dinner with a prayer.

One night, Pop handed around a "Family Covenant" card. "Because we believe that the use of alcoholic beverage is harmful to human personalities and to society, we, the members of this Family Circle, God helping us, hereby commit ourselves to total abstinence, and dedicate our home to creative fellowship and Christian service." We all signed, including Ruth, who was just old enough to write her name.

Mother allowed us one radio program an evening. My favorite was "Sergeant Preston of the Yukon and His Dog, King," a serial about battling wickedness in the frozen north. Bobby and I sat on the living-room rug with our ears a few feet from the speaker. When King was shot by claim jumpers and presumably killed, Bobby and I cried for hours and missed dinner. But King got better for the next evening's episode.

Late in the 1940s Pop bought a gigantic secondhand television that, through a mirror, reflected images of the Lone Ranger, Buster Crabbe, Bob Steele, Tom Mix, and

Howdy Doody. Later I watched the Army-McCarthy hearings on this TV and realized that Carl McIntire was right again. Something very important was happening in the world out there, but in this show it was hard to understand which side was God's—the army's or McCarthy's.

Some evenings, on his homemade record-maker, Pop recorded his children playing their musical instruments. He also recorded our first words, our birthday parties, and Pop's own recitations. "Trust and obey," Pop recited from the hymn of that title," for there's no other way to be happy in Jesus but to trust and obey."

When the newspapers headlined that momentous speeches were scheduled, Pop readied his record-maker by the radio. Here's Harry Truman announcing the first H-bomb test explosion: "The world will have peace through fear."

Later in the evening, as the older children did homework and the younger went to bed, Pop tinkered in the basement, often developing photos that he took of his family. Each Christmas, he and Mother mailed hundreds of Christmas cards featuring their three children. Or Pop fashioned useful articles such as the crutch he made when Mother broke two bones in her foot, or the hand electric generator that would light a small bulb or quiver a turtle.

Other nights Pop lay on the living-room couch reading and rereading the only nonprofessional books he ever read, *I Was A Pagan* or *Christ The Healer* or the Bible.

HIS SON

We were given baths by Mother who, as I grew older, instructed me to wash between my legs by myself, producing new mysteries. We dressed in our pajamas and Mother supervised evening prayers. "Now I lay me down to sleep. Pray the Lord my soul to keep. If I should die before I wake . . ."
I didn't know what a "layme" was and the thought that I might die made no sense.

Then I recited the Lord's Prayer and my personal requirements such as help in remembering twenty-eight prepositions for an English quiz, or penance for being bored in church, or opening my eyes while praying, or even thinking "damn," or accidently ripping a page of a Bible, or bumping a parent—the Bible said that parent-strikers were to be stoned to death without qualifications —or disobeying any of the Ten Commandments, including the ones I didn't understand like "Thou Shalt Have No Other Gods Before Me" (what did "Before" mean?) or "Thou Shalt Not Covet Thy Neighbor's Wife, or His Ass or His Manservant" (what did "Covet" mean?) or "Thou Shalt Not Commit Adultery" ("Adultery" was said so hesitantly by my parents that I wasn't about to ask them what it meant; just to pronounce the word out of Biblical context might be a sin).

In every evening prayer I asked God to destroy all the bars in the world and replace each with a church. That was a priority request. Pop assured us that nothing was worse than a bar.

I finished my prayers with "in Jesus' name," because

54

if I left that off I'd be praying like a Jew. I didn't know much about Jews—only one Jewish family lived on our block—but they were supposed to be different in some way. I didn't want to look like a Jew either. After the lights were out, I'd place two books on my prominent nose to flatten it while I slept.

In the night while the drum-major music-box lamp played "Twinkle, Twinkle Little Star," my brother and I held hands between our beds. This was our insurance against the dreaded man in the attic, or the dark presence in the cellar, or the bogie man lurking just outside our bedroom window in the lilac bush (the same bush that each spring filled our room with the fragrance of its blossoms).

A few steps down the hall Mom and Pop read the Bible to each other and said their own prayers before sleeping.

Their door was left open a crack so that Mother could hear our calls or cries. Once every night one of us would ask her for a glass of water and Mother, uncomplaining, would wake and bring the water. We were seldom really thirsty. We just wanted to be sure she was still there. Soothed, we would fall asleep again, listening to the distant clack-clack of the trolley to Philadelphia.

Long after her children were grown and no longer needed her to bring water in the night, her door was still left ajar. She still listened.

Saturday
and Sunday

ONE Saturday afternoon I was suddenly inspired. "Pull your sleds around me in a circle," I told the younger kids. They sat on their sleds and dug their galoshes into the snow while I told them that John 3, verse 16, said: "Whosoever believeth in me shall have eternal life," and that if they didn't believe in Jesus they would go to hell, and that it was important to go to church every Sunday. The six Mahoney kids didn't attend church at all, Pop informed me. I was particularly worried about them.

I told the kids we would meet every Saturday on our sleds in my backyard until all of them had accepted Jesus into their hearts. But next Saturday I found I had nothing new to say and we sledded off in search of more interesting play.

Our play may not have saved souls, but it banished

pain. Pammy Hicks, her sister, Bobby, and I took off our clothes and played doctor in a painless world with a plastic stethoscope and toy knee-thumper, until her mother charged up the stairs and ruined our magic. She found Bobby and me under the bed.

At Halloween we dressed up as the ghosts and bogeymen we feared and turned horror into laughter as we walked through the twilit neighborhood with Pop, collecting welcomes and treats.

But even at play, the world intruded. At the church's Strawberry Festival one Saturday, Bobby and I paid to see a cartoon show that was suddenly switched to an hour of *Victory at Sea,* a World War II documentary with flame throwers, mounds of bodies, and march music.

Pammy Hicks, who was two years older than me, laughed one Saturday, "You idiot! There's no Santa Claus, everybody knows that!" I ran across the street and told Mom the dumb thing Pammy just said. Quietly she admitted that they had lied to me: "Daddy is Santa Claus."

More confusion—a radio evangelist asked for money, so I put my allowance in an envelope, but Pop stopped me. He said I tithed at church and gave to Reverend McIntire too, and this evangelist wasn't a good one. Why not? He wouldn't say more. Were there good men of God and bad men of God, and how could I tell the difference?

In the Boy Scouts I learned how to lie.

Before a weekend camp in the woods, Pop told the

Scout master that he knew the Scouts were a religious group and that the Scout master would therefore conduct worship services on Sunday morning. The Scout master, a silly fellow with no serious intentions about anything, assured Pop that he himself would lead the ceremonies. But he didn't. On the way home, doing an illegal eighty miles an hour, he turned to me from his driver's seat and suggested I tell my dad a "little white lie." Were there good lies and bad lies? Wasn't lying always wrong?

I told Pop we sort of had church in the woods, meaning I had muttered a short prayer while hiking to inspect the muskrat traps. I prayed that we hadn't caught any muskrats.

Besides the art of lying, Boy Scouts taught me how to melt old records into candy dishes, how to make a wastebasket from a used ice-cream container, how to smoke a Kool's cigarette, how to "be prepared" for the disaster that was surely just ahead, and how to sing "Lady of Spain I adore you / Pull down your pants and I'll explore you."

Sundays at church it all became simple again.

Pop grew up near Oak Park Fourth United Presbyterian Church of Philadelphia and even when he married mother and moved to the suburbs, he drove to Oak Park—thirty miles round trip every Sunday morning for Sunday School and church services, and thirty miles again every Sunday night for hymn singing, and yet again every Wednesday night for prayer meeting.

When he finally moved too far out into the Main Line to commute, he joined the Bryn Mawr Presbyterian Church, but he was always uneasy with that church's wealthy congregation and more intellectual sermonizing.

I was taken to Oak Park when I was a month old. I graduated from the nursery, and the sandbox, and soon sat in the primary grade wearing my first tie, decorated with a Day-Glo flamingo.

On my sports coat was a Sunday School attendance pin with three bars on it, indicating five years of perfect attendance—a pin for the first year, a wreath around it for the second, and bars underneath for following years. My goal was the world's United Presbyterian Church record of forty-four years perfect attendance. That man's pin was framed on the church wall.

Primary school services began with a teacher's prayer and some hymns: "Jesus wants me for a Sunbeam, a Sunbeam, a Sunbeam / I'll be a Sunbeam for Him." Then we were asked to stand and recite a Bible verse we had been assigned to memorize last Sunday. For this we were graded on a wall chart with gold, silver, and blue stick-on stars.

Our teachers were kindly ladies who propped up a felt board on an easel and, with felt silhouettes and landscapes, told us the most extraordinary stories: about a wicked king that slaughtered all the male babies under two years old in an attempt to murder the Christ Child; about a kid who killed a giant with a slingshot and then cut off the giant's head; about a wise king who offered to chop a baby in half to discover who its real mother was. These ladies told us more pleasant tales too: about Saul on the road to Damascus and the sudden light that led him to Jesus—such a light flooded the living room one day and I knew Jesus had come to visit me, that it wasn't just sunshine poking from behind a cloud—and about Jesus in the temple, still a boy, teaching adults the Truth.

After years of Sunday School even the most gory stories became yesterday's news. Some of the bored kids sailed paper airplanes past the teacher and one boy heaved a hymnal across the room when he was scolded for failing to memorize all the books of the New Testament in order. Just in time we were graduated to Intermediary grade. A male teacher kept order.

Here I learned that I had not only sinned from time to time, but that I was a Sinner. "Mr. Mitchell, what do you mean we are all Sinners? I'm not!" I cried out.

"Yes you are, Billy. Every human is a Sinner."

What was the use of even trying to be good if you ended up in the same category as real sinners? Mr. Mitchell must have made a mistake about me and other good people. For instance, there were people who went to bars and there was me.

After Sunday School the family, led by Mother, walked down the church aisle to the second pew from the front. We sat up there because Mother said the minister would get lonely if everybody sat near the middle and back of the church. Also, Bobby, Ruth, and I tended to behave on display like that.

We drove home for Sunday dinner and then returned for evening hymn singing, where often I would play my coronet with Bobby on trombone and later Ruth on flute.

When I fell in love it was with the minister's daughter, Lois. She was quiet and shy with light brown hair that I exaggerated in fantasy to movie-star blonde. I couldn't think of a thing to talk to her about, and I was too light-headed whenever within ten feet of her to talk anyway.

One Sunday afternoon we went to the minister's house for dinner. I wandered into Lois's bedroom, found her there, and not knowing what else to do, sat next to her on the bed wordlessly. Pop and the minister looked into the room. "Oh they're . . . " Pop blurted. I bolted up and left the room, realizing I had done something too awful for Pop to mention.

I dreamed of Lois. In the dream we were together on a small bridge over a moonlit pond. I would swoon and fall into the pond.

I carried her photograph in my Roy Rogers wallet, and one night as Pop and I drove home from Sunday night hymn singing, I confessed to him that I was in love with Lois.

Pop said he had fallen in love once too, with Mom, and it was important to love only a good Christian woman.

For a few miles we were men in love together. It was the only time we ever talked about girls, about women.

Summer

I N the summer the evangelists came to Ocean City. Billy Graham pitched a big tent in a gravel parking lot. I sat in the back of the tent on a wooden folding chair next to Pop and heard this new preacher ask us to come forward for Jesus. But I didn't do it—I had already been saved that summer, twice.

The first time I was saved was at the Music Pier, a stucco building that jutted from the boardwalk into the sea and rested on eroding pilings. When the surf was rough I could feel the building shake.

Inside the hall, a visiting evangelist shouted from a platform decorated with potted palms about a Christian man who lapsed from the faith and began drinking and going with women. He stopped tithing and bought a

Jaguar sports car with his tithing money. The man knew God was angry with him and he promised God that he would reform and God listened to him and welcomed him back. But the man lapsed again, and begged forgiveness, and was forgiven, and then lapsed again. Finally God would not listen any more to his pleas. The man begged and begged but God had had it. The man parked his Jaguar on the Ben Franklin Bridge and jumped off.

At the end of the sermon, the evangelist asked all of us who wanted to be saved to raise our hands. I had thought I was saved from the day I put my hand on top of the radio, like Carl McIntire said to do, and said "I believe." But you couldn't be too sure about such things. I didn't want to end up like the man who stopped tithing.

The evangelist pointed around the room, counting hands and acknowledging salvations. I leaned forward in my seat and waved my hand so that he wouldn't miss me, and I looked over at Pop. Pop had his hand raised too. He smiled and nodded at me. I had pleased him greatly and I was glad.

Outside on the boardwalk—surrounded by vacationers in shorts sucking on ice-cream cones and frozen custard, pushing baby carriages and trailing balloons, banging at pin-ball machines and blasting rifles at metal ducks—I felt exactly how I had been told I was supposed to feel. I was pounds lighter. My sins had been lifted from me. I was floating. I was certain that the crowd could see me floating.

"Saved!" I wanted to shout as we walked down the

boardwalk toward home. And now Pop and I would save the whole world! This was no ordinary Saturday night stroll. This was a march, a march to banish sickness and pain and evil and war from the world and bring in Jesus Christ. Holding Pop's hand, I wanted to put my other arm around everybody on the boardwalk. Pop and I were marching for Jesus and we'd conquer the continents for Him.

The next morning I felt just as light and sin-free. But I was a little worried. Had the evangelist really seen my hand? It was a small hand. I was a small boy. Perhaps he'd missed my hand in the crowd. If he had, was I saved for sure?

Sunday evenings Pop sometimes took me to the Baptist Church. The four sides of its short steeple announced in red neon to the town below "Jesus Saves." I liked the evening services here because they showed the missionary society's movies of unsaved Hindus worshiping cows, and walking through burning coals. Being a Christian was obviously better than that, and I had a mission to change such foolishness.

Summer Wednesdays I attended a Vacation Bible School in the basement of the Baptist Church. Here a frantic high-school girl taught Bible stories to a class of ten children. She often took us to the beach to play stick ball and interrupted our games to ask us to kneel in the sand and pray to Jesus together. She said she wanted to save us. All we had to do was raise our hands. I knelt in the sand in my bathing suit and raised my hand. She promised me that this time I was saved for sure.

Mom supervised the play of summer days while Pop worked here and there for GE. After breakfast Bob and I, and later Ruth, would scrub the dishes and perhaps help run the wash through the wringer and pin clothes on the clothesline in the yard. At eleven o'clock sharp we gathered the beach umbrella, and old inner tube, buckets, and shovels and walked to the beach. After Mom coated us with Gaby suntan lotion, we constructed ornate sand castles, sand forts, and ball runs, or dammed up tidal gullies or battled each other on our rafts in the surf or met new kids who became instant friends.

Jesus was far from my mind.

Mom would knit or read *McCalls* or *Ladies' Home Journal* (they were discovering "togetherness" for families) or talk with the other mothers. At one o'clock she unwrapped the sandwiches she had brought and gave us money for half-pint cartons of milk at Big John's beach stand. In the late afternoon we walked home, my brother and I squabbling over whose turn it was to carry what. We showered in an outside shower, hung our suits out to dry, and after dinner listened to a Phillies game from Philadelphia or read books like *Nobody's Boy* or *Paddle to the Sea,* with the constant sea sounds two blocks away.

Pop drove down on Friday nights, carrying the week's mail and some new magazines for us to page through. On Saturday the family went to the beach together and on weekend nights we visited a lagoon to feed stale bread to wild ducks or treated ourselves to five-cent ice-cream cones or parked at the airport to watch small planes take off and land.

On Sundays we went to various churches. I liked to sit near a window where I could observe the sinful people walking to the beach when they should have been in church. But perhaps they were Catholics. Perhaps they had gone to Mass early, or on Saturday night even, as Catholics did. They were wrong, of course, just as the priests who vacationed next door to us were wrong to drink beer—Bobby and I found the empty cans in their trash and wondered what kind of sinning went on in a house of beer-drinking priests. Even if these beachgoers had been to church, they were still sinning. Pop never let us go to the beach on Sunday. I think he was uneasy about the beach even on Saturday. He alone wore his swimsuit top even though the fashion had changed.

Some Sunday mornings we visited the Ocean City Tabernacle, a huge wooden auditorium, and heard visiting ministers. A minister from Princeton Theological Seminary said a few Bible stories were just myths, but they were still important myths.

We never heard such heresy at Dr. Fisher's First Presbyterian Church of Ocean City, a stone building with permanent pews and paid professional singers named Nancy Fishburn, Tommy Perkins, and Fritz Kreiger. They bellowed operatic solos, duets, and trios in front of a two-story stained-glass tableau of Jesus praying on a rock in Gethsemane. A light from heaven shone on His face and changed each time the outdoor light changed, an indication of God's mood, I thought. There was no air-conditioning. We beat the air with cardboard fans decorated with a scene from the Last Supper and advertising a local funeral home. Because of Dr. Fisher's thick German accent I understood few of his sermons, but Pop seemed to approve.

Sunday evenings, the Ocean City movie theaters were transformed into houses of God. Pop and Mom allowed us to see only one movie a summer and I often felt a sinful tingle as we walked under the marquees advertising romances and adventures to hear even more visiting evangelists and ministers tell us that Jesus was coming soon.

Once a summer Pop took his two-week vacation and on one day in that vacation he rented a rowboat and we went fishing. Mom would get seasick halfway through the day and Pop would leave her off on an island in Great Egg Harbor Bay while we anchored offshore, properly life-jacketed, and kept on fishing.

Pop could never bring himself to stick a hook through a minnow for bait. He used clams instead, and rather than breaking their shells open with a hammer and cutting them up, he bought frozen, pre-chopped clams. He let the fish we caught die slowly on the bottom of the boat because he could not bear to take more direct measures.

"Watch the fish hooks!" "Watch the fish hooks!" he would warn us, afraid that we would hook ourselves.

Years later I would complain to him that his life had been run with that fish-hooks motto, but all I really noticed those summers was that Pop was a hero, rowing against the tide, blowing his plastic whistle at speedboats that came too close, retrieving Mom safely from her island.

Pop performed other summer wonders too, like shingling the whole Ocean City house up to the roof. I tried to help, but I got dizzy a little way up the ladder. Pop actually clambered to the ridgepole.

He said that wasn't so amazing. He said he had climbed hundreds of feet up the sides of buildings and storage tanks for GE.

I saw him doing it for God.

Being Good

IN junior high school, the gym coach, Crusty Diller, said the new seventh-grade boys would be expected to comport themselves like men. This meant doing pushups, situps, rope-climbing, football with tackling, and taking a shower with the other boys. Crusty wanted us to be men, and naked.

Naked? For me to be naked with other boys watching was to exhibit myself as a freak. I had changed in a way that no other boy had even begun to change. I was odd in an unspeakable area of my body. I knew it was unspeakable because no adult ever spoke about it. So I broke Mr. Diller's rules, kept my underpants on at all times, and hoped he wouldn't notice that I hadn't showered.

I couldn't ask the other boys what was happening to me. They'd talk and make it worse than it was. How could I ask them what I suspected I was supposed to know already?

The boys knew other secrets too, like the meaning of "wack off" and "necking" and "making out" and how it was a great sexual conquest to discover a kid's mother's first name and then yell it across the playground: "Dorothy!" or "Black Dot!" They scored on me, and sent slips of paper around the classroom, smirking at the single black spot of ink.

I acted as if I understood.

As to the act itself, I concluded it was like pissing. There'd be this cheerleader standing where the urinal was, with an an ankle-length black dress that flew up to reveal orange and black school-color underpants and . . . But occasional wet dreams told me that sex was not like pissing. It was something else.

According to Pop, the Big Sin was drink. But at thirteen, I had no urge to drink. I knew it would send me to hell, and it didn't seem like much fun anyway. So one night with my mind on the Big Sin, I gave Ruth a quarter to show me what a girl was like. Neither of us thought we had committed adultery. (I wouldn't notice Ruth again for years, until the first time she wore stockings to church. Then she remembers Bob and me laughing at her.)

I tried so hard to be a man in Crusty Diller's terms that I developed a hernia. Now I was doubly freakish: hair and a hernia.

Before going off to be examined for the hernia, I spent hours clipping hairs with fingernail scissors until I was sure the doctor wouldn't notice. The doctor confirmed the hernia and shouted to my mother in the next room, "My God, he's shaved his pubes!" My mother, with more manners than him, said nothing. The doctor assured me I needed an immediate operation, that it could only get worse.

I promised God that I'd do just about anything for Him if He'd fix the problem. That week I hit a grand-slam homerun during lunch-hour recess and ripped my gut so badly I couldn't walk for three days. On the fourth day, the hernia was healed.

In silence, Pop drove me to my first date. He parked outside of Edie's house and I rang the doorbell and met her parents and Edie got in the car between Pop and me and shook hands with Pop. We drove to the Suburban Theater to see *The House of Wax* in 3-D. After we put on our special glasses, I reached my arm around her chair. Edie leaned forward. I acted as if I didn't notice her leaning. We watched a woman stripped and encased in hot wax. She became a wax statue. Edie leaned forward until the movie was over.

I called Pop to come and pick us up, and while we were waiting outside I tried a joke.

"Let's get married," I said.

Edie laughed.

I interpreted this as my first achievement with a girl.

71

So I said it again, and Edie laughed again, only this time not so loud. The third time Edie looked bored and stared down the road for her ride home, and when it came, we got in the car, I walked her to the door, and then Pop and I drove home in silence.

Edie asked me to a party at another girl's house. Both Edie and the girl were said to be pretty and popular, so I accepted. It was important to me that a girl have a reputation as pretty and popular.

I didn't understand what made a girl pretty. Being blonde like Marilyn Monroe might. If the boys said a girl was pretty, I accepted that, even if she was decorated with pimples and braces.

And if she was a cheerleader or a class officer, then she was popular. To have a cheerleader nod to me in the hall was to have a good day; to have her stop to talk with me was to be destined for greatness.

Edie was class secretary.

After she invited me to the party, it got around that we were going steady. I liked that rumor. It proved I was becoming popular, and wasn't that what girls were for? To make you popular? It was all part of the grading system. Maybe even of the Permanent Record itself. God, my parents, teachers, and other kids were watching me, and I was doing just fine because Edie invited me to the party.

At the party, my eyes teared when I tried to talk. All of the other couples disappeared into the two cars parked in the garage. Word drifted back that they were making out.

Edie and I sat alone in the rec room reading magazines. I wondered if I was supposed to ask her to make out, and how I'd ask that, and what you did if you were making out.

But she never asked me to another party and the rumors about us stopped and for a time I didn't have to worry about making out.

I had faith that if I worked hard, got A's and B's, was elected to some class office, did extracurricular work, stayed out of detention, and struggled to succeed at the hernia-threatening quarter mile for the track team, a girl would be mine, a really popular, really pretty girl.

Near the end of ninth grade most of us paid a dollar to become members of the Little Acorn Society, where one Friday night a month we danced in a large room to 45's.

It was no longer so simple, this being good. Boys and girls hung around outside smoking cigarettes. I had heard that some of the girls were letting themselves be ''felt up.'' More shocking were the jokes that boys told girls. Girls weren't supposed to hear those jokes.

Most disturbing of all, I noticed that my friend John Gilette, class president, was becoming friends with a kid named Bud Olson, who was flunking subjects left and right and who had actually been arrested for beating up a younger, Jewish boy. John seemed to prefer Bud's com-

73

pany to mine. And girls liked Bud—and two D-average football players named Hudner and Laiser—lots better than me.

I went over to John. "You've changed," I said, my voice breaking, near tears. "Why are you friends with Olson?" John Gilette didn't say anything. Later on, I saw him and Olson laughing. They stood looking at me from across the room and I stood waiting for the dance to be over so I could call Pop to pick me up.

Nature

"WHAT does it mean to be alive?" I asked myself one day in seventh-grade science class. I meant the difference between me, alive, and a rock, dead. But I was immediately amazed and disturbed. What kind of a question was that?

If I went home and asked Pop, he would have said "Aw, come on." He would have been just as embarrassed as I was.

The Bible taught that it was wrong to think too much. Look what happened to Doubting Thomas for all his thinking. Or the Three Wise Men. They ended up on their knees next to a cradle.

Pop's church had the answers. No questions were needed.

75

Pop was planning to move our family from Penn Wynne, just outside of Philadelphia, to Bryn Mawr, ten miles to the west. I asked him to find a place with lots of woods and a stream. I wanted to build a fort in the woods.

Pop found just the place, and while the house was going up, I was banging my fort together out of leftover lumber in a mulberry tree.

Swaying in my tree fort, I worshipped God in the clouds, in the sunrises and sunsets, in the stars. The minister's and Pop's prayers often praised the "Glories of Thy Nature" and I basked in those glories. God was not in cities. He was here, speaking to me. I prayed to Him that President Eisenhower and Comrade Khrushchev would not blow up His creation.

Meanwhile there were problems to be solved under the fort. That's where you had a deadly contest between good and evil, a contest I could do something about.

The oak trees were strong. I decided that they were therefore good. I also decided that they were being treated unfairly by certain faster-growing, weaker and ignoble trees, like the silver maple, for example. Oaks grew about six inches a year, whereas the weak silver maple could do two feet or better in as much time.

I took sides. I scouted the woods for oak seedlings, and I transplanted them on the borders of Pop's property, slashing down weeds and silver maples to make a space and let the sunlight through.

I lectured to Pop about the value of strength, and as

a hurricane approached during our first autumn in the house, I orated to him about cutting down the huge silver maple on our front lawn. Did he admire weakness? Why couldn't he bring himself to hurt a tree? Did he doubt my judgment? Because I wasn't going to sleep in my bedroom under some silver maple during the storm. So I slept in the living room while the wind toppled trees and the power failed. But the silver maple tree survived.

There were good and bad animals under my fort too. Predators, like foxes and crows, were evil—and those they preyed on, such as rabbits and pheasants, were good. In the junior-high print shop I worked up bold posters that proclaimed NO HUNTING and under that PREDATOR HUNTING IS OK, and I signed them: "The Henderson Game Commission."

The woods behind our house were private property, but I posted the signs on trees for miles.

I hunted myself—righteously, of course. My mongrel dog, Duke, and I hiked through God's woods in search of the devious fox (which we never saw) or the nestling-devouring, egg-sucking crow. Duke chased anything that moved, mostly rabbits and pheasants. But he was so clumsy that rabbits ran through his legs and pheasants shot up under his chin and tumbled him over. Duke was good for laughs all around, I figured.

I hunted with a slingshot loaded with unripe wild grapes. The crows hawed at me from the sky as I called to them with my crow-caller and shot hard fruit at them.

But, like Pop, I couldn't abide suffering. He couldn't

prune the berserk arms of his fruit trees, and I couldn't make more than feeble passes at crows, post dopey declarations, and build a huge brush pile under my mulberry tree where rabbits, pheasants, and other helpless nobilities could run and hide.

But the greatest of all evils was man's attitude toward the snake. The snake was not slimy, as believed, most were not poisonous, all snakes were terrified of people, they could not roll up in a hoop and attack us, and what's more, snakes were our friends—because snakes ate our enemies, the vermin. It was horrible how people killed snakes for no good reason. So I set out on a one-man campaign to rescue the reputation of the snake. In our eighth-grade public-speaking contest, my holy vigor carried me from a classroom appearance to an address before the entire school.

I won second prize.

I expected that my communion with God's Nature would lead to a forestry career, and then I would become United States secretary of agriculture and after that . . .

In a speculative autobiography written on assignment for English class, I reflected, "They sure have been a great and colorful sixty-five years . . . Now as secretary of agriculture I am thinking of running for the presidency of my country. If I win or lose makes no difference because I consider my life a success from every point of view."

The Size
of the Fight
in the Dog

To Principal Edward Holyoke Snow our education was a war game.

Snow's favorite slogan, which the entire school, teachers included, chanted at pep rallies was: "It's not the size of the dog in the fight, it's the size of the fight in the dog." On his orders we concluded each day standing beside our desks while a lone trumpet sounded taps in the hall, a tribute to America's war dead.

When Ardmore Junior High School opened in 1923, Ed Snow was named first principal and for thirty-three years he had prowled the halls of the two-story building, a six-foot 300-pound, crew-cut, firm-jawed man in school-colored orange and black tie and socks, his silver whistle swinging from his neck.

The whistle was Snow's gun. By fondling it in a noisy school assembly or by pointing it at a misbehaving kid, he would get instant obedience. And when he actually blew it, followed by his outraged bellow, students shivered and the object of his noise cringed and awaited his judgment. Snow's whistle was no respecter of child, teacher, or God—he'd even blow it in the halls during the morning devotion period, showing a discourtesy to God that I wondered about, and then hastily forgot. One didn't question Ed Snow.

Ed Snow rehearsed us in his war games by assembling his troops in the auditorium for any excuse and haranguing us on the evils of pegged pants and d.a. haircuts; on the glories of Roger Bannister's first sub–four-minute mile; on obliterating our rival, Upper Darby Junior High School, in every sport.

Snow had created our arch rival and detested enemy out of his head and for three decades he had assured ''his babies'' that there were few greater dishonors than losing to Upper Darby, a larger and tougher (poorer) school than ours.

''It's not the size of the dog . . .'' he'd start and we'd yell after him.

Out of hundreds of faces, none escaped Snow. He'd stop the cheering and blow his whistle through a megaphone. ''That one! You're just mumbling! Get to my office!''

Then he'd get on with the cheering, hurling his bulk into the air next to the cheerleaders.

Snow's *Ardmore Junior High School Handbook* was my first experience with secular philosophy. It was issued in a new edition each year and included everything we needed to know, from the specific ("All eating is to be done in the cafeteria") to the general.

Snow's *Handbook* confirmed to me that my first question about the meaning of being alive might not have been so embarrassing afterall. Here were other deep thoughts about life such as "On the plains of desolation bleach the bones of countless millions who at the moment of victory sat down to rest and resting died."

Or mysteriously, "All but the dead left the field."

Unlike other teachers who stuck to the curriculum, Ed Snow told us only what he believed. Life was a battle. The just men must win and they will if they don't give up. Communism, lying, cowardice, cheating, sneakiness, and sex were bad.

Snow was quite open about his sex phobia. As a prize for drumming up the most magazine subscriptions for his War Memorial College Scholarship fund, he bused the top-ten sellers (I was third) to the movie *Battle Cry*.

Unfortunately, he hadn't seen the movie and didn't know that some scenes took place in a whorehouse. I thought they were just friendly ladies. Snow apologized to the school and advised that we boycott the movie.

Since Snow had reached the mandatory retirement age of sixty-five, we were his last class and he doubled his energies in demanding that "my babies," as he called us, become American Men, proud of our school's and country's traditions. (He had few direct words on American women.)

If there wasn't a handy tradition around he made one up: the annual Spoon and Chain Ceremony had been concocted by Snow from a seven-foot wooden spoon attached to a heavy brass chain. Each year the ninth-grade class officers were required to drag the spoon and chain onto the stage and hand them to the officers of the eighth grade, symbolizing the passing of "school tradition and spirit" to the next class.

Snow also dreamed up the school mascot, the leopard ("fearless and tenacious"), and the Mace, a silver artifact that sat on the school officers' table during chapel indicating through two entwined snakes the "united cooperative authority of the faculty and student body." But the snakes never got to cooperate. It was Snow's authority completely.

Snow said that the School Gavel, wielded by the student-council president, was constructed from wood taken from the ship *Constitution* and from Independence Hall. I never understood how he lifted the wood from either place legally.

Snow's most popular tradition was his annual Christmas story, "Capping the Main Truck." Even though we all knew how it ended after his first telling, Snow orated his tale to high suspense. A fourteen-year-old boy in a Maine seacoast town (where Snow grew up) was required to prove he had become a man by climbing to the top of a ship's main mast and hanging his cap at the peak. Until he achieved this, no boy was allowed to go to sea. Snow never admitted he was the boy in his tale but we all imagined he was and he didn't discourage us. For fifteen minutes every Christmas we were with little Ed Snow as he struggled up that mast, hands slippery with fright, almost falling at the first, second, and third yardarms, and finally arriving at the main truck—the disk near the top that the halyards ran through. The ritual did not permit that the boy climb through the truck on the rungs provided; he had to crawl out and around the truck a hundred feet over the deck. Slowly the boy inched around the truck, dizzy and trying not to look down. With his last strength, he shinnied to the peak and capped the mast, a man at last.

Not long after Snow's final Christmas story, the fervor about his retirement began. We all chipped in—no kid would have dared refuse—to buy him a red, green, and white tail-finned DeSoto and a trip to Bermuda for his wife, himself, and their retarded daughter—all of whom showed up on stage for the tearful presentation assembly.

Ed Snow lived to see most of his boys and girls into early middle age—in a world with standards of behavior that Ed Snow never imagined any world would have. He died well into his eighties, honored by a community he had amazed.

Pop's ministers had always said it was *what* and *who* you loved that made the difference between heaven and hell, success and failure. I was afraid. I was afraid that even men like Ed Snow were oaks and Pop was a silver maple.

Later Pop would say outloud about himself what he had hinted at then: I'm nobody to pay attention to.

I looked for other heroes and my love for Pop ended. For years I did not return his affection or touch him. Only his angry slap would have made physical contact between us. But Pop, unlike Mom, never hit me in anger, and his one accidental slap brought him near tears with apology.

When Pop's father died, I mumbled that I was sorry about that, but I didn't go to the funeral. I wanted no part of even funeral sympathy with a silver maple.

Job's Boils

SOME mornings my face was so run over with pimples that I begged to stay home from school. Even on the best days, it was a question of which side I should keep to the hall wall or in the shadows at recess.

In more hopeful moments I was proud of my pimples. I was sure this was just another sign that I was special because God was putting me to a test. Like Job. All things worked together for the good of those who loved the inscrutable Lord.

But at other moments I wasn't so sure that God hadn't gone as berserk as my spreading acne. The foods I needed to succeed—like honey for energy in the quarter mile—made a mess of my face. This was an awful conflict. Didn't God want success? He wasn't making sense.

When Clearasil failed, Mom took me to the doctor.

He said that Vitamin A was a new sure-fire cure. He prescribed massive doses, promising relief in three weeks. In three weeks the pimples were still flourishing, and my hands and ankles had broken out in a rash of warts.

We tried another doctor. He burned the warts off.

But disasters built character. Look what happened to Abe Lincoln, a minister said one Sunday. Abe's life was a series of calamities—including being fired from his first job. When I was fired from my first job, at Klein's Ocean City Supermarket, after only three days, I figured this was like pimples, a test of my spiritual stamina.

I went out and got another job at a boardwalk hot-dog stand.

Whenever I failed to win a school office, or whenever the in-crowd didn't invite me to parties, I figured it was merely because of the pimples. They'd go away some day. In the meantime I studied, got straight A's and never thought I was a "hard up"—a kid that was left out of things.

I started borrowing styles.

From the popular boys, those who had "personality," I borrowed dirty buck shoes (the white bucks that Pat Boone inspired were too flashy for me), semipegged pants, Alligator brand jerseys (never red because red highlighted my pimples), and a semi-d.a. hair style, swept back but not gathered into a true duck's ass. We college-bound types thought the full d.a. like Elvis Presley wore was too lower class.

Once I had made a popular girl laugh when she bumped into me on the stairs. Picking up her books, I blurted "Don't step on my blue-suede fingernails," borrowing from a song then in vogue. The remark came out of nowhere, and it made no sense. But for some reason the girl howled. I hadn't slept well the night before. I decided lack of sleep was the secret of winning wit.

Yet future efforts at fatigued wit didn't work at all. I panicked in conversations. My eyes teared. Through experimenting, I discovered that too much sleep was just as wit-reducing as too little. I calculated that the correct amount of slumber was between eight hours and fifteen minutes and eight hours and twenty minutes. I became a fanatic about getting just that much.

Harvey Ford, football captain and perennial class president, was stony silent, expressionless. I never saw him happy, sad, eager, anything. The girls said his silence proved Harvey Ford was profound, and the boys, myself included, said sure—and tough too.

I tried to imitate Harvey Ford's unresponsiveness. But my eyes gave me away. They watered and my voice shook when I was nervous.

In ninth grade, Harvey Ford was out of school for three weeks, hospitalized for high blood pressure.

John Gilette, who alternated with Ford as Student Senate president from year to year, projected a combination of friendliness and seriousness. I practiced John's trick of looking a person in the eye. But that got my own eyes tearing all the faster and I had to look at my feet.

George Riggs was a tall, skinny blond kid. And he had this laugh that started low and rose to a scream. The girls were crazy about him. I figured the laugh was why, so I practiced it in the summer before ninth grade began. This would be my year, I thought. My pimples were clearing up. With George Riggs's laugh I'd play the romantic lead.

Dressed in my new complexion, in my new red Alligator jersey, in my semipegged khakis and freshly brushed dirty bucks, topped by a perfectly combed Vitalis-controlled semi-d.a., I moved to the center of a co-ed group on the morning of the first day. As they swapped tales of summer, I waited for the right moment. I waited. Then I unleashed my new laugh.

The girls stared. They looked at each other. They walked away.

This time it wasn't the pimples.

I tried again. I hit them with that laugh.

This time the boys walked away too.

I'd seen how George Riggs had a way of stomping his right foot hard while jitterbugging. I thought I could use that to good advantage. At the first rainy-day noontime dance, I went slamming around the gym. I thought I was a sensation.

Ninth grade! I knew this was my first big year.

The student nominating committee put me up against Richard Vianni for class treasurer.

Vianni was a short, aggressive boy who delighted in

whispering "Black Dot" whenever he met me in the halls. He was said to cheat on tests. Morally and physically I counted him no match.

The class treasurer's office was a hokey faculty creation. The only thing you did was read the treasurer's report at class meetings, a report prepared by a teacher. But Richie Vianni and I went at it in precise imitation of the Eisenhower-Stevenson campaign.

With Mr. Snow inflaming us, Vianni and I plastered the building with our campaign signs. "Bill's Best" or just "Vianni" in a streamer of letters. We intrigued among ninth-grade boys for a campaign speaker. I picked one, only to fire him at the last minute when I schemed that my speaker must not speak but instead sing my praises. Tommie John had been on Ted Mack's Amateur Hour on national TV, and Tommie John was a school hero. The night before the election, I called him and read him the words I'd written for him to sing—to the melody of *Jingle Bells:* "Vote for Bill, vote for Bill, he's the best today . . ."

Vianni and I stayed outside the auditorium while his speaker and my singer addressed the class. A half hour later, a ballot counter walked into geography class and congratulated Vianni on his victory. Worse still, Vianni whipped around in his seat and shook my hand across the aisle.

Perhaps I failed because I lacked loyalty. God was telling me I shouldn't have fired my speaker for a singer.

In the summer of 1956 I read a book about Paul Whiteman and the Big Band era. I formed a dance band—me
on cornet, my brother, Bob, on trombone, a drummer,
and two saxophonists. I planned a break for the big time,
with me out in front, Paul Whiteman.

I called our first practice session, made a peppy
speech, told them our name was The Continentals, and
handed out the sheet music. We worked on "You Always
Hurt the One You Love" and "Beat Me Daddy Eight to
the Bar." Then I called a break for a short touch football
scrimmage in the street, and we never got back to our
instruments.

No matter, We Continentals had natural talent. No
need to practice.

I entered us in the Ardmore Junior High Talent Contest. I painted a big CONTINENTALS sign to prop over us,
and then one day we trooped up on stage after a ringing
Tommie John introduction. Mother was in the audience
—as she was for all of her children's grand moments.

I gave the nod and Bob and I began "You Always
Hurt The One You Love." But the other fellows thought
the first song was "Beat Me Daddy Eight to the Bar." By
the time we heard what they were playing, the audience
had already heard too much.

After having tried for two years to win one quarter-mile
race, I knew ninth grade was my year to star. I asked the
coach to start me alone because the only kid who consist-
ently beat me was on our own team. The coach agreed,

and at the gun I sprinted off and had built up a large lead at the 220 mark. With only one hundred yards to go, I heard the coach yell, "Look out!" as four kids from the other team bounded by me. I made a feeble kick to the finish line and then got down on my hands and knees and threw up.

Maybe socially this was the year. I would give the first party and that meant that everybody I invited would have to invite me to their party.

Pop was enthusiastic about Bill "having his friends in." He spent evenings painting the basement floor, whitewashing the basement walls, and enclosing his workshop with wallboard.

I carefully assembled a list of the kids I thought were in the in-crowd and mailed my invitations.

Mom made punch and baked cupcakes and had hot dogs and hamburgers ready. Pop and I spent that Saturday afternoon hanging balloons and crepe paper in the basement. When I moved two chairs into his wall-boarded workshop, he said, "None of that," and dragged them out.

"But, Pop, we have to. Everybody does it," I said.

The chairs stayed out.

"It" was "make out in the MO room." My party would be branded for hard-ups if it ever got out that I didn't have MO facilities.

I was worried that nobody would come. But they did. In no time at all, the in-kids were jitterbugging to recordings by Bill Haley and the Comets. Even George

Riggs was there, banging his foot on my cement floor. Trembling, I moved two chairs into Pop's workshop. A couple followed. Another couple got two chairs and went into the room after the first couple. When Pop came down the cellar stairs with a tray of warm hamburgers, he saw the chairs gone, the door shut. "None of that," he said and routed out the make-outs. He turned on his workshop light, took the chairs out, and went back up the stairs.

George Riggs yelled, "This party is for hard-ups!" and smashed his fist through Pop's new wallboard.

I wasn't invited to any of the in-parties. In fact, I went to only two parties all year, and I had to invite myself to both of them. What was worse, things were suddenly getting so murky that I couldn't figure out just who the in-crowd was: kids who swore, smoked, and flunked were hanging out with class officers, cheerleaders, and honor students.

So where, then, was the reason for my spectacular failures?

Be good Pop had always said. It followed that the reason I was getting nowhere was because I had *not* been good. I had seen defects and, instead of condemning them, I had tried them on for size. Not until the end of the year did I complain to John Gilette, and, later, to Harvey Ford, about their tolerance for immorality and their new friends: Ron Dominic, who had actually been in jail; Bud Olson, who beat up the Jewish kid; and Betsey

Trees, who told dirty jokes, drank beer, and once said to me "I like to bang until my belly hurts."

Appalled and stricken, I stood by as Barbara Meyer, straight-A student and vice-president of the school, started going steady with big mean Jim Laiser, center for the football team and a D-average dimwit.

I decided to be good again. And since Pop never said exactly what he meant—"if you don't know what Good means I can't tell you," he said—I'd have to guess. But this time it was going to be for keeps.

It was going to be all the way for me, for Pop, for God.

The Virtue Chart

I learned about Ben Franklin's virtue chart in a Personal Growth leaflet sent to me from the Government Printing Office in Washington, D.C. It was one of dozens of leaflets I ordered from a catalogue that included titles like *Ten Ways to Become A Winning Public Speaker* or *You and Your Teeth.*

I found that many of my virtues were the same ones Ben Franklin was interested in, and, like him, I expected practical results. I also expected that someday my biographers would be interested in my chart. At Franklin's suggestion, I marked myself every night with pluses and minuses and totaled up the score in the various virtues at the end of each week. I did best in Moderation, Loyalty, Non-Boasting, Justice, and Industry, and not so good in Tranquility.

It was from Ben Franklin that I learned about a virtue I'd never thought of before.

Meditation.

Meditation was an important virtue, and I took care of it each night in a window alcove off my bedroom that I had turned into a meditation chamber. The alcove was just big enough for an old kitchen table, a chair, and me. I strung a wire and hung a sheet across the alcove entrance to shield it from the bedroom I shared with Bob.

Bob said nothing, as he watched the closed curtain. To me, Bob was a shadowy annoyance whom I would meet as a friend only years later.

In order to score proper marks in Meditation I had to read at least one Personal Growth leaflet and a chapter from the Bible each night, plus enter my ratings on my Virtue Chart. After that, I would turn out the light, open the window wide no matter how cold the weather, and gaze at the stars. I knew God was out there. I would reach out to the sky to touch Him. I expected that one night He would touch me back.

Once Pop opened the bedroom door to say good night, and he saw me reaching to the stars. He didn't say anything, and I didn't either. "Aw, cut that out, Bill," he said finally. I didn't reply.

Pop watched me for a while. I could tell. And then he shut the door.

It was in this alcove that I quite by accident discovered another virtue. I noticed I could produce the most remarkable feelings, actually transport myself into ecstasy, with attention to my crotch. I hadn't imagined that my body could feel as wonderful as this, so transfixed. It had to be a sin.

Each week I graded myself worse and worse in a category I called "SD" (a meaningless code for what I was trying not to do. I didn't want my biographers to know my shame). I listed this virtue, SD, under the general heading of Bodily Clean, a class of virtues that included a bath on Monday, Wednesday, and Saturday; clean toenails and fingernails; three full glasses of water a day, and combing my hair.

I became so upset with flunking SD that I flunked myself in the entire Virtue Chart at each week's end. But I couldn't give up the chart, I thought, because I had to grade myself. I didn't trust anybody else's grades—not the church's, not the school's.

Each night I would climb into bed and pray in despair that God would help me stop. And then I asked him to bless Mom and Pop and Bob and Ruth and President Eisenhower.

And then I wacked off.

Rings

Years before, at Oak Park Fourth Presbyterian Church, Mom and Pop bought me a ten-dollar membership in the I Am His Society. I received an embossed certificate announcing that I had been admitted into a Special Society of the Saved, a society dedicated to lifetime missionary work for Christ. I also got a thin silver ring inscribed with the initials IAH.

I put the ring in my dresser drawer and forgot about it. But in the summer of tenth grade, just after being hired for my second job as a boardwalk hot-dog slinger at Mike's Hole In The Wall luncheonette, I found the ring and put it on.

It's not that the ring had some religious significance for me. What it had was something else that I wanted—

something solid, to remind me not of *Him,* but of *me.*
When my eyes watered and my voice shook, I would
look down at that ring through the tears. I'd see it, and
it would remind me never to stop believing in me. To be
strong. To buck up. Because I was having trouble remembering who I was. Lots of trouble.

I was stealing from Mike. Each morning when I
opened up the Hole In The Wall, I would swipe a ten-cent
bottle of Welch's grape drink and a slice of Wonder
Bread. I covered the bread with catsup, washed it all
down with the grape drink, and then I'd hide the bottle
in the bottom of a trash barrel before Mike and his wife
arrived.

Mike was suspicious of everybody, and it wasn't
long before he discovered my thefts. He told me to cut
it out. But I knew he couldn't afford to fire me because
he was paying me half the minimum wage. Mainly what
I worried about was his telling Pop.

So I worried. But not too much.

I realized it was impossible for me ever to turn entirely
from the church. I would never do such a thing. Of
course! In fact, I still walked on the beach at dawn deliv-
ering sermons to myself. "Don't ever forget God!" I
yelled at the ocean. "No matter what happens!" I
pounded my fist into my palm.

I was beginning a journal and wrote in it each night
instead of marking my Virtue Chart.

Page 137 said: "On leaving the church, the intellectual is liable to, and probably will, forget the established law of God. So don't leave the church!" Page 140 said: "Never forget you are the son of a King. UK."

The "UK" was my code for unknown attribution, which meant me.

Around Labor Day, a girl from school saw me cooking hot dogs at Mike's. She sat down at a stool to ask me how my summer had been.

I said, "I am tearing down truth block by block and I'll build it up again the same way."

"That's nice," she said.

I put the IAH ring back in my drawer and bought a more substantial ring, flashy and chrome-plated with a turquoise-colored glass stone. It cost me $1.50 at a board-walk five-and-ten.

It was truly my ring.

I called it The Ring of Myself.

What confidence I didn't get by looking at The Ring of Myself I tried to achieve in high-school power games.

As for Pop, he let God take care of the power thing. The idea of being near any power but God's made Pop nervous. He'd laugh nervously when he mentioned inviting the minister of Bryn Mawr Presbyterian Church to dinner. *Too powerful for the likes of me,* was Pop's unspoken message.

But I decided power and who had that power and how they used it was important. It was a lesson I'd learned from Carl McIntire. Now it was my turn for power.

In high school, power was extracurricular activities. So I applied for and was named drum major of the Lower Merion High School All-Boy Marching Band.

In my maroon-and-white drum major's uniform with the gold braid and trim and the three-foot-high white-rabbit fur hat, I took up my position at the head of the band. With a whistle blast, I announced the start of the half-time show during football games. That was power. That was Ed Snow. Then I'd shout and do some fancy gestures with my big silver baton. As thousands of Saturday fans watched, I led the band downfield with a determined and flamboyant duck-footed strut.

Talk about stomping one foot when you jitterbugged!

Pop regularly showed up at weekend games to photograph me in uniform for the family album.

When in tenth grade I won my first elective office as home-room rep to the Student Senate, the victory had little to do with my performance on the Virtue Chart and much to do with scheming.

I had delivered an impassioned campaign speech on the "sunlight of knowledge," proposing, along the way, that we each establish a pen-pal international understanding relationship with an Australian student (a relationship I already had), and then I mailed Christmas cards to every member of the home-room.

I later won re-election through the success of my various projects. Like the Marriage Booth at the all-school Orphan's Home Charity Fair. I made myself a minister and, for two dollars a couple, I performed the ceremonies. The teachers complained that the booth was sacrilegious and they openly worried that certain couples might consummate their fake vows. But I convinced them it was for a good cause.

I listed the rules of power on paper.

"A leader should associate with those under him on business terms, rarely on social terms."

"A command should be given sternly but never resort to anger. Force often will beget force and hatred of the leader."

"Press ever onward, not showing your deeds ostentatiously."

"There should be a gap between classes, not in the showing of love, but in generally understood mutual terms."

"Don't holler. Smile and bide your time."

I briefly connived for the presidency of the Student Senate. But I blew my chances by leaking my plans to a friend, who told his friend, who wanted the job too, who told everyone else what my plans were. Too available, too crooked, I was not nominated. I had to settle for editor-in-chief of the new school newspaper, which I had to found in order to be editor-in-chief. I declared its banner "Toward Thought and Humor," and laced the thing with my essays on reason, nuclear war, the New Youth, world peace, and shallow suburbanites.

I was so busy being a powerful person that I gave myself cause to worry about neglecting my truth search. With real agony, I wondered if I were demeaning my soul by dressing well for my editor-in-chief's job. Would Christ have worn a tie?

I turned to Dale Carnegie's *How to Win Friends and Influence People,* to get the lowdown on his rules for leadership: *"Seem* modest." "Develop a personal trade mark like a red tie." "To size up a man, ask questions when he is off guard."

I copied them down in my journal. But when I looked and saw them there, they really disgusted me. I crossed them all out and scribbled STINKS at the head of each page.

I was becoming bored with lurching down the football field in a rabbit hat, bored with plotting to hold school office. So I got myself excited about the Anticommunist League. There'd be this inner core of us dedicated freedom-lovers who would do anything, even kill our own grandmothers, for freedom. And then a semi-core of less-trusted freedom-lovers, and then the masses themselves in the outer core, lots of people taking directions from us in the inner.

"We must not banish but learn to live with the A-bomb!" I proposed.

But then I graduated from politics and decided to invent a no-stick Band-Aid, or an air spray that dampened hay-fever pollen so it would fall to the floor. I set about writing a play in which two beatnik lovers commit suicide.

I started changing horses fast, whereas Pop still rode the ox of his God. I saw him plodding onward, straight and true. But his lesson did not help.

Love

Pop counseled me to love only a Christian woman, but other men thought differently.

Eighty-five-year-old Bill Booth, the boardwalk super-intendent, wore a sea captain's cap and an official badge from the Ocean City police department. His job was to yell at shirtless men strolling on the public thoroughfares and to blow his whistle at bicyclists riding the boards after curfew. Other than that, Bill Booth had little to do, and so he would drop into the drugstore where I clerked during the summer before eleventh grade selling sundries and sneaking peeks into the paperbacks that filled the racks.

My favorite was *How to Make a Million Dollars.*

To me Bill Booth was the law, upholder of morality, the type of fellow who kept our standards high in that resort. Also, he was a family patriarch—six children, fifteen grandchildren. So it was to him that I brought my complaint about the gift shop three doors down the walk.

The shop was displaying in the window a large beach towel, and it pictured a woman holding a tray, on which there rested her tremendous bosoms. The towel was captioned: *I got these melons in Ocean City, New Jersey.*

"Can't we close that shop down?" I complained to Bill Booth.

Mr. Booth eyed me from under his captain's cap, trying to determine if I was serious, I suppose.

"Pretty nice pair of jugs, if you ask me," he said.

In the summer of 1957 I wanted only to be in love . . . and to have the other kids know I was in love.

Her name was Ellen. She had a summer house nearby, and she'd newly entered my school, same class.

One Saturday in August, Ellen and I took a bus to Atlantic City and danced to Stan Kenton's band at Steel Pier. On the way back, the bus driver dimmed the interior lights and I put my arm around Ellen. I tried to draw her close but got nowhere, and finally I was willing to settle for a kiss on her cheek.

Another day, we sped out into Great Egg Harbor Bay in the Sears kit runabout that Pop and I had assembled.

I cut off the Johnson 5-hp outboard and we drifted in the sun. She let me play with her hair. That seemed okay— real progress. And her hair was blonde.

At the end of August she invited me to the Lifeguards' Ball, and I got very sunburned beforehand, because I'd read somewhere that swarthy men were sexy. I brought Ellen a corsage, and we walked up the boardwalk to the ball eating a bunch of grapes. It was my most romantic experience with a girl ever. But that night Ellen told me she was going back to her steady boy friend when school opened again. She said she couldn't see me anymore.

For a year that covered it for me and true love. I carried the torch for Ellen where my sorrow would do me the most public good.

I tried to find the basic psychological premises for a love affair: "Be nice, but don't get so mushy and girllike —be a man, you know, *tough,*" I scribbled in my journal.

"Don't let a woman get away with anything. No weakness," I quoted the advice of a classmate.

I contrived elaborate plans for wooing a girl—watching her, studying her interests and her reactions to other boys, plotting to meet her needs. But none of these ever worked.

"Try a little tenderness." I got that from a popular song, and it forced me into a reversal from my be-tough period. I tried to exhibit powerful indications of tenderness. It didn't work so hot, either.

Then I learned from Will Durant's *Story of Philoso-*

phy that Schopenhauer doubted the use of the entire effort: "Love is a deception practiced by nature to cover up reproduction." I copied this wisdom into my journal.

I tried my mainstay—the Bible, the place where Pop's guidance had its source. First Corinthians 16, verse 13, said: "Watch ye, stand fast in the faith and quit you like men." Since my opinion of the faith was less enthusiastic now, all that was left to me was quitting myself like a man, whatever quitting meant.

But then I read where Emerson said "To be a man, you must be a nonconformist," so I wrote an essay attacking the shallow beliefs of contemporary Christians, and read it aloud in school.

Pop didn't know what to say about my manly antichurch nonconformity. But I did. I said: "Pop, people don't respect a man who doesn't stand up for his own ideals."

I expected that lots and lots of girls were going to be impressed by the new Emersonian me. Except they weren't, not a one.

"The diamond cannot be polished without friction, nor the man perfected without trial." It was an old Chinese proverb. I wrote it on a slip of paper and carried it around in my wallet. I would refer to it every once in a while and keep my courage up.

I looked a lot, but I couldn't find one other nonconformist in the eleventh grade. Well, not exactly. Actually, there was a girl who was known to read poetry and paint pictures. So I asked her out. Betty Howard. She talked nonstop and sneered at school spirit. I sneered at school spirit too, and swore that if this date didn't work out I would give up on girls forever.

My first date with Betty was also the first time that Pop didn't have to chauffeur. I was sixteen and had my license. We went to a movie and then parked for hours in the Pontiac outside of the apartment house where she lived with her divorced father.

We talked about poetry and Jack Kerouac.

I decided I didn't care if she was fat and nothing to brag about back at school. Here was a girl who loved to read books and think deeply.

I invited her to my house the next day to read my journals. She read all of them, and I could see she was doing it with great care. She even commented in the margins: *Great!* or *Wow!* After my cynical "Sometimes it is necessary to be insincere," she wrote "Think again about this."

She gave me her paperback copy of Jack London's *Martin Eden,* with red underlinings of her favorite passages and *Tremendous soul!* or *What a poet!* in the margins.

The next Saturday, we went to another movie, and, afterward, we drove to Valley Forge. We parked under the Observation Tower and kissed, and she suggested that we climb to the top of the tower and experience Valley Forge's historical tradition in the moonlight, and write a poem.

We climbed over the locked gate with the warning about trespassing and walked the steps to the top. We hadn't started our poem, or even begun to experience the moonlit tradition yet, when a police cruiser pulled up down below and began poking around my car.

"Up here!" I called.

The cop picked us out with his spotlight.

"We're writing a poem!" I shouted down.

Driving home, Betty and I planned our great court-room battles and composed our speeches about how poetry transcended petty laws and about how poets should be allowed to experience Valley Forge after hours. To us that cop was a symbol of the barbarian world out there. It was the two of us against the millions of them. Like Thoreau, we would go to jail before we'd give up our inmost beings to rules favoring property.

For weeks, we eagerly awaited our court summons. But it never came.

One night we drove to a distant town to hear Louis Armstrong. On the way, Betty told me all about jazz, who was good and who was great. When we got there, we stood at the edge of the dance floor, and shouted at Armstrong between numbers. "Hey, man, what you got in that cup?" Betty yelled up to the stage as Armstrong swigged from a tin cup.

"Just water, honey," the great man assured her.

Jazz, poetry, fiction, philosophy—Betty had them all

under her belt. I could see there'd never be another girl that knew what Betty knew.

After the Armstrong concert, we walked to the car holding hands, and I reached in my pocket and took out the I Am His ring. I fitted it onto Betty's finger.

"I want you to have this," I said. "It doesn't mean anything shallow, like we are going steady or any of that. But I just want to give it to you."

She put her arm around my neck and said, "Ahh."

Inside the car, I ran my hand as far up her leg as she allowed.

I went to Ocean City for the summer. I didn't expect to see Betty again until the fall. But one day she telephoned me at the drugstore to say she had a mother's-helper job in Ocean City. The job was for a week, she said, and then she said *she would be alone in the house the first night.*

Could I come to see her when I got off work?

I said I'd be there—at midnight.

At midnight, we went for a walk on the beach, and thought about all the other thinkers who had paced the sands pondering the deeper meaning of life. Then we went back to the house. I telephoned Pop and said I was starting right back with the car. Betty got into her pajamas and kissed me good night.

That did it. She took off her pajama top, but stopped me when I tried to peel off her bottoms. We went to her bedroom and lay with my fingers hooked in her bottoms. We listened to the surf. If the church was right, this meant Hell. But I decided I'd risk it. I yanked on her bottoms again.

"Oh, okay," she sighed and stripped them off.

But that stopped it. After twelve hours at the store, I was tired. I wasn't getting anywhere except scared.

The phone rang. I looked at the clock. It was three A.M. We had been trying this for two hours and I had no excuses for Mom or Pop, and it was one or the other on the other end of the phone. So I didn't let Betty answer it.

I kissed her good night, very commandingly. I told her not to worry. It was a sin, I said, but maybe it was natural. I didn't know what I was talking about—what I wanted to do or what I couldn't do. I'd never heard the word impotence.

I was ten blocks from home when I saw a lone figure walking toward me—Mom. She was hiking the entire fifty-five blocks to get me.

I stopped the car and opened the door for her. She bit her lip and stared ahead. "Honest, Mom, nothing happened," I was able to say with some truth.

At home Pop pretended to be asleep. He said nothing the next day, either. In fact, he never did. But he must have complained to Mom plenty. He did that when he couldn't confront us.

Mom handed me a little booklet with two pages of

111

information about sexual intercourse and twenty-two pages about syphilis and gonorrhea.

A month later Betty and I finished what we had started. But then she got hysterical and concocted a douche of Clorox. I got hysterical too. I thought I heard her father at the apartment door. So I kicked the screen from the window and readied myself for a three-story leap.

Every night afterward we consoled each other by phone. I promised Betty that when she had the baby we would go live at the seashore beneath the whispering pines. I promised we'd write poetry and read books forever.

But Betty didn't have a baby. She gained more weight and began to babble and laugh in shouts. Then she dropped out of school and told me she tried to kill herself with an overdose of Bromo-Seltzer.

In my journal I wrote: "Betty is far from lost and has tremendous potential. I resolve never to give up on her improvement."

But what about Truth? Was this love play just frivolity? No. "Sex is natural and therefore part of truth," I wrote.

I resumed my search for the deeper meaning of life without Betty.

My next girl friend was not a poet or a philosopher. She was president of the high school's chapter of Future Nurses of America. In fact, her father, a vice-president of a box manufacturing company, informed me that poets and philosophers were useless, and that if I admired such types I should stay away from his Bonnie. But Bonnie assured him that I was really regular, and went with me, anyway—for a while.

I was tired of thinking.

I'd had it with soul.

Bonnie and I did it now and then, scrambling around in the front seat of the Pontiac, or in the grass. I did it without guilt, without thought of hell or adultery. I did it for fun. Together, we tried to discover what a blow job was and only got as far as her taking deep breaths and doing some sexy puffing.

In the end, her father won. My hair was too long, and my inclinations uncertain.

Bonnie wouldn't visit me that summer. So I was stuck with reading *Lady Chatterly's Lover* and wandering the boardwalk of that Christian resort trying to come up with a line for the girls.

I wondered if I was becoming a menace.

I worked off my frustration on a twenty-five-page tablet that I titled *My Philosophy of Life*.

On page one, I scotch-taped a news photo of a Chinese boy begging for rice. Across from him, I taped a photo of a rich American lady in a new feather hat that, according to the caption, cost $200. Then I wrote: "Most men can be convinced by reason to renounce their narrow outlook. But women will forever cling to their stupid Hollywood, Narcissistic, Lipstick, Cosmetic, Child and

Home and Gossip worship. It is my firm conviction that women, guided by the selfish stupidity of Madison Avenue and the materialistic outlooks of our business-bound country, are ruining any promise the U.S. ever had of leading the world to a new respect for the individual and freedom from the need to conform like slaves.''

I left *My Philosophy of Life* lying around where I thought Pop might find it. It never occurred to me to think Mom might.

Truths

I N the summer of 1958 I put Beethoven's Fifth Symphony on the record player. It seemed something I ought to do, to get to know classical music. It was a duty.

But unexpectedly the symphony lifted me from the couch in joy. I didn't know music could do this, certainly not classical music.

That summer I discovered all of Beethoven's symphonies. I read Kant, Spinoza, Nietzsche, à Kempis, Locke. If I didn't understand, it didn't matter. I read to be reading.

Such enthusiasms set me apart not only from Pop but from my two pals, Ernie and Tex. We were Saturday sporting buddies—touch football in the fall, driveway basketball in winter, baseball in the spring, with Cokes and horsing-around afterward. But one Saturday in Bryn

Mawr when Tex and Ernie arrived on their bikes at my house, I removed myself to the record-player upstairs, turned on Beethoven's Ninth extra loud, and yelled down that I didn't want to hack around and the rest of it. I wanted to listen to Beethoven!

It would be years before I had male friends again.

As for my brother, Bob, I either ignored him or tried to beat him up. (Bob remembers that once he thought to take a log to the back of my skull, but dropped the log in mid-swing and ran into the house to pray it out with Mom and Pop.)

Pop's father—the other male in our family—sat through the last of his eighty-six years in our summer house. The rest of the time he lived in a nursing home.

Like his son, Grandpop was silent. He moved only to light a White Owl or shamble to the sun on the porch. He said nothing of his life or Pop's.

I made contact with him once. On separate radios, he in the living room, me in my bedroom, we listened to the Phillies game from Philadelphia. They were contenders for the pennant and they were behind. "Swish" Nicholson hit a pinch triple in the bottom of the ninth and won the game for the Whiz Kids. "Grandpop!" I yelled and bounded down the stairs to pat his shoulder. "He did it! Big Swish did it!"

Grandpop smiled and nodded at the radio.

I wanted to grab Grandpop and dance.

"Yes," he said. "He did it."

Through his ministers, Pop had inspired in me a vision of

116

God's grandeur. But now it seemed to me Pop had no notion at all of that grandeur. While Pop lay on the sofa downstairs holding his hernia and reading *Christ the Healer* over and over, I sat in the meditation alcove upstairs taking notes on Schweitzer's *Search for the Historical Jesus.*

I learned that the Gospels didn't agree about Jesus, that they were written a century after His death. This was amazing news and something that Pop never mentioned. Maybe Pop didn't even know it!

I began to address my family the way Reverend McIntire addressed people.

Mom suffered this with her usual grace.

I detested math courses and to get me through algebra and geometry, she tutored me every night at the kitchen table while I complained to her—a former math teacher—that all math was useless.

"It helps you think and be logical," she said.

"Logical!" I'd holler. "You call yourself logical? You call Pop logical? I don't want to solve any crummy algebra problems! I want to solve the problems of life!"

She stayed calm enough for both of us, and in the end we got the problems done.

I postured like a Jeremiah, attacking my parents for their attention to lawn-cutting and to their savings account (savings to send me to college). I sermonized to them about their fellow church members who dared to drive up to the abode of the humble Christ in chauffeured Rolls-Royces.

The teachers were "shallow and materialistic." I even found that the fifties' teenage literary hero, Jack Kerouac, was more or less lacking. I wrote: *"On the Road* is a story of bohemian life—an unending poem of joy at being alive. But Kerouac's heroes don't think about other people at all, and this is most outstandingly wrong."

People were to be thought about seriously. That's what I said. What I did was something else.

At dinner, I'd finish eating in a few minutes and spend the rest of the meal on the floor, moaning "I'm bored, bored, bored."

Pop would look down at me beside him. "Ah, come on, Bill, get up."

Unable to fathom me, Pop turned his anger on Bob. (Bob sat at Pop's left hand.) Bob had passed six feet in height by age fourteen and he was still growing.

Pop would turn to him and say, "How come you keep getting so tall. Can't you stop?"

Pop would ask the same questions night after night.

But mainly Pop escaped to the basement, where he'd repair a radio or tinker with something, or talk on the phone for hours with his brother Clarence. They talked about the Communist menace and the advisability of a sneak nuclear attack on Russia.

Clarence thought we should bomb them right away before they got any stronger.

Pop wasn't sure.

But in matters of religion, Pop was sure. He believed in the inevitability of hell for nonbelievers. He couldn't stand to give a tree pain by pruning it, or to slap his sons, but Pop was sure that God burned people eternally. The question once came up. Mom suggested it was a symbolic burning. Pop said, no, no, hell was real, people really burned there. On the other hand, Pop couldn't imagine anybody he knew—including his arrogant son—roasting in hell. Pop was sure that, in their heart of hearts, the worst people believed in Jesus and were saved.

Our tenth-grade Geometry teacher required us to memorize a Thought for the Week, and tested us on the Thought each Friday as part of the regular geometry quiz.

"Show me a man who has made no mistakes and I will show you a man who has done nothing" or "Tell me who your friends are, and I will tell you who you are."

I added these Thoughts to my journals. My idea was: "The best policy is to have one. You won't be confused in any situation if you have a policy for everything."

The ministers had made it seem simple in Sunday sermons. And simple it was: life was a matter of mottoes, arrived at by anybody in serious search.

I also recorded my first deep conversation with a Jewish student: "To get to heaven in Judaism you must be a descendant of one of the favored tribes of Jews. Three of these tribes intermarried with pagans and have lost their right to heaven. There is now room in heaven for only 36,000 descendants. Another requirement is that you do more good in life than bad. Christ is not the savior for many reasons. The most glaring of these is that the

Old Testament states after He comes there will be peace."

All this is quoted and not necessarily true, I added, as if to clear my record of his error.

After homework, I entered such thoughts in my journal. Then I opened the alcove window and reached out my hand.

Philosophy Club

I hate the clouds. They hold down my soaring vision," I blurted when Carol Saunders telephoned me.

I didn't know her. I didn't understand why she had called. So I babbled something nervous.

Carol Saunders said she thought my statement was poetic.

We began to discuss poetry, philosophy, music. Every night on the telephone we covered the three of them in just that order—poetry, philosophy, music.

We figured kids like us should stick together. So we formed an exclusive club, the Main Line Philosophy Club, Carol and me and a half-dozen other boys. They may have arrived expecting sexual favors from Carol, who was rumored to let herself be "felt up."

The existence or nonexistence of God was our topic week after week. Now and then we touched on communism and ethics. But what we wanted to settle was Was He or Wasn't He.

We scored points on Carol's living-room floor, often not assessing arguments so much as the lack of intelligence of the speaker.

"You just fell ten points on my list," a class brain informed me after I'd defended God's existence with a quote from the *Reader's Digest.*

Some of them dropped Hegel, Marx, and Wittgenstein into the debate. I doubt if they had actually read the books, but to protect myself against my ignorance of philosophers I hadn't read I bought a paperback titled *Philosophy Made Simple.* It outlined dozens of thinkers in a few paragraphs each. When confronted, I'd excuse myself to another room, check out *Philosophy Made Simple,* and then rush back with a retort.

Most of the kids proclaimed themselves to be agnostics and a few said they were atheists. It was I alone who defended God's certain existence with my six points, the best of which was the last one:

6) Only God could have thought up the plan of Christ dying on the cross. That perfection should die in torture must be God's idea.

Anyway, the Philosophy Club argued and argued about the existence of God until we argued ourselves blue. One kid brought a six-pack and told us he'd rather stay high all day than think. We played records and danced.

Young Life, an evangelical youth group, heard about us and concluded the club required conversion. We were invited to a face-to-face confrontation by the Young Life leader, who would speak for Jesus, whereas a boy named Gay Wilson, a straight-A math student who had scored early acceptance at MIT, would defend God's nonexistence.

Here's what Gay said—boiled down to his six points:

1) There is no God because the emotions of religion can be removed from the brain by depriving it of certain chemicals.

2) Everything in the universe that exists can be proven to exist. Not so with God.

3) The search for God is just a father hunt.

4) If God exists, why is there so much misery in the world?

5) Man is even now creating a virus and soon will make soulless, intelligent life.

6) Since the universe has always existed, there is no need to think about a Creator.

From the sidelines, I shouted out refutations. (Imagine the universe always existing! The magnitude of this new idea stumped me.) But I was growing tired of my own six points. I was growing tired of the Philosophy Club.

So I thought up a new club, the Thoreau Club.

We'd assemble in a small room at the very top of the high school. The Thoreau Club would be limited to those who *really* understood. But I never made it very clear to myself or anybody else what it was that they would really understand.

But I do remember that around this time I was very fond of the phrase, "the soul of nature."

In a way, I suppose, I was coming close to worrying about the possible agony of trees.

Reason

AFTER one of my regular tirades at the dinner table, Pop said, "Bill, why don't you go out for track again? You were happier when you ran the quarter-mile."

I dove off my chair and announced my most recent theory from the dining-room rug. "Happiness isn't the point! Rationality is! What did God give us our brains for but to use, Pop!"

Logic was my path to the Truth, and it was also the key to society's organization. I wrote in my journal: "Citizens must be smart to be logical. Therefore, sterilize all men and women with an IQ under 110. This is one way, if not *the* way, to produce a truly free society not dominated by dictators, the church, or Madison Avenue."

As editor-in-chief of the school newspaper, *The*

Forum, I proclaimed the New Age of Reason. I wrote: "The New Age has dawned. The sunlight of a new generation of youth is about to flood the landscape of wars and disease, jealousies and hypocrisies. We will have no dogma. We will abolish instinct and mass stupidity by the reasoning of the new youth."

As to my role in the New Age of Reason, I mused in my journal: "Could I possibly be the bit of dust to realize the dreams of thousands of pain- and hunger-stricken men? Could I move this mountain? The thought terrifies me. But I will try. My God, I will try until I drop dead!"

Meanwhile, I no longer stuck "In Jesus' name" on to the end of my nightly prayers. But that was just more Reason. I believed in a God of all religions, not just Jesus' God.

More significantly, I didn't open the alcove window at night and reach out to God in the stars. Instead, I lay flat on my back in bed and thrust my hand to the ceiling. I figured if God was God, He would find me here.

Only once did I lose it all.

Maybe God really *was not.* I'd never thought about it seriously. But now I did. He didn't exist, and neither did Truth.

"How bored you'd be if you ever found Truth. What else would there be to do . . . and besides maybe Truth is just a personal thing."

If that was so, then I was out of a job as a future prophet. Billions of personal ideas must be tolerated. "O

Compassion," I scribbled, with more despair than compassion.

I woke up at night horrified.

But after a week of this, I suddenly realized the fault of atheism. It was irrational. It wasn't *getting* me anywhere.

What was the *use* of it all.

None.

Having solved that problem, I began to marvel at what other kids knew, for instance Carol's friend Tad, who once worked in a hospital and had seen real death.

I wrote: "August 16, 1959. Tad and I talked about death. When you are dying the mouth suddenly goes limp like a fish's mouth; then the eyes, which may have been staring in terror, continue to stare but slowly glaze over. Then you are dead."

Fathers

HAMILTON COLLEGE was a men's college in farm country, on top of a hill, miles from the nearest city. I intended to live like a monk on that hill.

I spoke to few people and studied constantly. Other students thought my silence meant strength, depth, and leadership—the old Harvey Ford success syndrome. Somebody nominated me for Freshman Council and I won the election. It left me cold. Politics was behind me, I had promised myself. At Council meetings, directed by the associate dean—who indicated his authority with snappy openings and closings of his cigarette lighter—I sat in a corner and said nothing.

Only beanies brought me to action. When the sophomores enforced the wearing of beanies by freshmen during the first semester, I aimed a loudspeaker at the quad through a dormitory window. "Freshmen, burn your beanies! If you give in to the sophomore tyrants, you will give in to the Communists too!"

For nights and nights I yelled that from the window. But I made sure it was somebody else's room.

Later, in an attempt to be reasonable and direct as a man should be, I went to the head of the sophomore honor society, who was responsible for directing the beanie-wearing tradition. I told him how the beanies resembled the stars imposed on Jews by Nazis.

He smiled and thanked me for the visit.

The next week, after compulsory Tuesday chapel, I was grabbed from behind by four sophomores and hustled down the chapel steps, my books scattering behind me. While eight hundred men jeered and the dean smiled indulgently, I was crowned with a baby bonnet and forced to wear a sign around my neck. "Baby" it said. I was both crucified and honored.

My daily monk's outfit was a T-shirt, khaki pants, and a leather jacket. Because of my dress and indifference to campus activities, I was dubbed "Skid Row." One night while I was in the library, a kid swiped my journals from my room. Every night after that there would be a reading in the halls—Skid Row's Search for Truth.

"Skid Row" they'd shout at me from dormitory windows. I developed a case of shingles. It didn't clear up until I threatened to punch the guy who'd been reciting my journals.

I was sick, desperate, and alone, and still trying to learn how to think. What was the first premise?

My roommate's father, a navy admiral in charge of submarine atomic missiles, had a premise—Love. What did love have to do with the missiles? I asked. He said we needed missiles until we got peace and then we'd find love.

"Love" I wrote in my journal.

I was writing in the journal every day now, whether I had an important notation or not. Thoughts came and went and often I'd try to run my life on the Truth of the previous day. Some days Logic was the key; on others Emotion was everything. "I feel therefore I am," I proclaimed after meeting Tom Bruno, a junior.

Tom Bruno was a jazz pianist, a midnight yodeler, and his favorite expression was "Wow! Oh Wow!"

His fraternity house, Emerson Literary Society, was the only house interested in my membership. ELS thought I was a rare literary sort. When I mocked their attempts to impress me with a dinner in a fancy restaurant, they liked me even more.

In Bruno's emotional outbursts, in his flouting of standard conduct, I found a hero. We hitchhiked throughout New York state to girls' schools, often in snowstorms, rideless, drunk, howling back at farm dogs, and quoting Nietzsche to each other. I loved Bruno like a father and said so outloud, to the great amusement of everyone.

"Want another Bru?" they'd raise their glasses to me

at the ELS bar. It was a line that went around when I was nearby.

I didn't know how to act without imitating Tom Bruno. I was shouting, "Wow! Oh Wow!" That was the way I *felt*. That was the truth.

I let my hair grow. I announced I liked it long "so I can feel it blow in the wind."

I waited for a full moon, climbed a hillside, stripped naked in the December night and masturbated at the universe to force it to see the truth of me. "I am! I am!" I hollered into the silence. But when I came I forgot what the point was in the first place, and I fell down into the frozen cornstalks, disappointed.

I broke up with Bonnie. Her father refused to let me see her unless I got a haircut first.

I did, but it didn't do any good. Bonnie said her father was right—I was too wild, too crazy, and this was our last date. I made a production out of it, kissing her pubis goodbye at her front door while "the cold wind rushed up my leg" (it was halfway out the storm door) and then speeding to Ocean City and tramping along the ice-covered boardwalk yelling the names of people I had known the summers before, particularly old Mr. Booth, who had just died.

"I am alive, alive, alive!"

I waded into the ocean and thrilled at the pain-truth of the cold. "Alive!" I screamed.

A cop spotted my car, whistled me up from the

beach, and ran a check of my credentials, my trunk, and an estimate of my sobriety.

"I am drunk on life," I told him. He stared at me and left with a shrug. I drove home laughing out loud at all these pathetic attempts to stifle my truth, my self!

I wrote: "Never before have I known the reality of my life so clearly. I am not dead. I am alive! Oh Wow!"

Amy Rose, a spring houseparty date, and the black-haired daughter of a New York psychiatrist, was also Mad for Life—and Mad for It. Until then I had to persuade a girl to do it. If they performed, they performed reluctantly. But Amy Rose didn't care when, where, or how. We snuck into the dorm after hours or dragged a sleeping bag out to the golf course and I would write in my journals that "our bodies rippled by the rippling stream."

Amy Rose shrieked without shame, clawed my back until it bled, and begged me to come inside of her. "Fuck the consequences!" she demanded. She was also the first girl I knew who said such words.

For a month and a half we were together every weekend. She paid my train fare to her "Park Avenue apartment"—it was on East Eightieth Street, off of Park, but that was close enough for my romantic notions about addresses. Amy Rose was my "Amy Flower from Park Avenue," and I was delirious about the "big city" and my rich, long-eyelashed, long-fingernailed, fashionably skinny girl friend. (I later found out she had a serious disease of the throat and couldn't swallow properly, so that's why she was so skinny.)

"I love her," I recorded in my journals. "The dream has been fulfilled!"

When Mom and Pop came up to Hamilton for a visit, I greeted them with an arm slung around Amy Rose and a can of beer in my hand.

Pop said, "You don't drink, do you, Bill? I know you don't because you signed the family pledge."

They drove us to Philadelphia. Amy and I sat in the back, held hands, kissed, and wrote notes to each other. At my house, we did it on the bathroom floor while Pop called from downstairs, "Bill, come out of there!"

The next day I took Amy to the Philadelphia Art Museum and she just disappeared. It turned out she had gone back to New York. No explanation.

I wrote in my journal: "The sensuality we experienced was just beginning to reach its climax when we parted. In a warm shower, standing up, etc. Let me always remember her freedom from any sexual ethic save our own pleasure. But marriage to her would have been impossible, and jail even worse." (She was only sixteen and I worried for some weeks after she disappeared that she might have gone back to New York and turned me in for statutory rape.)

That semester the dean of students declared I was an "underachiever."

"Oh Wow!" I laughed.

Tom Bruno went to work for his father in an upstate New York grocery that summer. I got a job as a newspaper reporter in Ocean City.

One morning it occurred to me that feeling was just one of the truths of the self. Confusion. But no matter—"I will make up a Faith in the Void," I promised, excited by the possibilities for that faith—mystic, stoic, egotist, Christian, anything is possible.

But I picked up a dentist's daughter on the Atlantic City boardwalk and forgot about faith for a while.

She was an Ohio State student from Coatesville, Pa., and her friends called her Crunch. I marveled at her white breasts constrasting with her dark tan, at her sassy, confident manner, and at her wonderful interest in me.

Crunch and I decided to live together for the rest of the summer—nine days. We hit the road by bus. First we visited Carol of the Philosophy Club in Wildwood and that night Carol and her boy friend and Crunch and I constructed a cross, doused it with gasoline, lit it, and tried to float the thing down a river. I have no idea why we thought this was so funny. But the cross tipped over and fizzled out immediately.

"Crunch is by far the most intelligent girl I have met. She is an artist, a poet, and will major in journalism," I wrote.

Then we went to Newark. We got a room in the New Belmont Hotel, a declining establishment where our love could bask under the sunny smiles of the manager, Uncle

Sam, who didn't bother to ask the dreaded question about marital status.

Then her period started.

That meant no sex, right? We looked at each other and wondered what we would do now. Nothing. The great odyssey was over. We spent all our money on two big meals and prepared to break up. Then we found out what to do about it—so we stayed together a few more days and promised to write each other during the fall.

We did, and I sent her my fraternity pin, which meant that we were now pinned, which meant engaged to be engaged.

Life was good.

From time to time, I would remind myself that I still hadn't discovered the truth yet. I jotted down remarks about how even if we couldn't know God we still had to make choices and that was the really terrible thing— because God just might be angry about our choices.

I decided for some reason that I hated Crunch. I never told her because I didn't understand my hate. Then she telephoned to tell me she loved me as never before. I hung up the phone and cried. I had realized something about God. He was hated by the people He loved. I felt awful about the loneliness of that unknown God.

The handwriting in my journal started getting sloppy.

Over the Christmas break, I drove to Coatesville and found that since our last meeting Crunch's face had broken out in a rash. She announced that her father didn't approve of her being pinned to a non-Jewish boy, and that he wanted her to break it off. At a party I drank myself into idiocy and woke up on the couch in her family's small apartment listening to her father complaining about me from the breakfast nook. "Why us? Why us? Why us?" Crunch and I agreed on a trial separation.

Back at college, I joined the wolf pack, fellows, usually drunk, who risked their lives to drive hours down the icy thruway to the nearest girls' schools. We swaggered into the dorms of Vassar with real fear and hate, brushing unattractive "ughmoes" aside, looking for beauty and love.

The leader of the pack was Woodward Flagler, a tall, skinny, pimple-faced kid who had discovered Allen Ginsberg, who had invited him to spend a weekend on campus teaching, and who had actually raised the money to pay Ginsberg. When one of Flagler's professors expressed reservations about Ginsberg's ideas in a panel debate, Flagler boycotted the professor's class for the rest of the semester and still got an A. The faculty treated Flagler not as a student, not as an equal, but as a superior. To me, and others, he was a god, a new father.

Woody announced to us that he was a Renaissance man. We didn't know what that was. But Woody, reclining in his throne—a plastic lawn chair, the only furniture in his room—said he intended to be an authority on everything, beginning with the jazz that his stereo blared, to movies and art and philosophy and technology and nuclear physics. The universe was Woody's, just as it had been Pop's through his God. I was seeing an authority I'd seen before.

When Woody paraded into the lounges of girls' school dorms at the head of the pack, unshaved, his red hair uncombed, wearing his black basketball sneakers, and more than once sporting the tops of his pajamas, he created instant theater. Women who were at first amused or made nervous by Woody's zaniness were quickly bullied by the zealotry in his glaring eyes and his demanding voice.

Woody would instruct on any topic and often quoted Ginsberg: "Grace, Love, Community." He also let his pack know which women were beautiful and which were to be ignored. He understood beauty in women and art. I didn't. I obeyed.

Woody's power was not confined to campus.

He and I took a government class field-trip to Washington. On our tour Woody brought along his ever-present bag of popcorn. He would down several bags of popcorn a day and unceremoniously regurgitate as much as he could of it—an act of defiance and bravado. He did just this on the White House lawn.

He swaggered through visits to Jerry Ford, a leader of the House of Representatives at the time, and with Jimmy Hoffa. Woody took over the conversation from the stammering government professor who was our tour tutor, and conducted the discussions with Ford and Hoffa on his own terms. He was most impressed with Hoffa, who said power was everything, and either you had it or you didn't, big people and little people. Woody said, yeah, that was the way the world worked.

I didn't dare ask him what Ginsberg would say. I didn't want to lose Woody's friendship by seeming critical. He was touchy and quick to rage.

That night Woody took on an entire theater watching *Tea and Sympathy.* "This is sentimental bullshit!" he hooted and threw popcorn at the screen. I dragged him from the theater when a burly fellow threatened to get tough. Woody unsuccessfully tried to break a Coke bottle to fight him with.

We were boarding at the home of a representative from Ulster County. That night Woody collared the representative and informed him that his political future in the county was quits, unless he listened up to Woody Flagler, who had been a summer reporter for a Kingston newspaper. I noticed that the representative listened to Woody for half an hour, asking questions and soliciting advice.

In campus politics Woody was rising fast, even among those who despised him for his slovenliness and his belching and farting. Woody was elected to two terms as TKE fraternity president, demanded and won from the dean the right of agnostics to avoid compulsory chapel, and organized with Mark Marshall, one of three campus blacks, the picketing of a hotel chain for their racial discrimination. His and Mark's demonstration made national headlines, was featured on all three network TV news programs, and helped start all the civil-rights demonstrations and student uprisings from 1961 on.

For art class I attempted a self-portrait in oil paint. I had always wanted to look like a thoughtful person. In my high-school yearbook I had posed gazing into the distance mystically, much as I imagined Thoreau did. The effect was a glassy-eyed stare suggestive of narcotic stupor. Now, for my art class self-portrait I paid particular attention to the eyes—glaring, no nonsense. I hung the finished portrait on my wall, thinking it was a fine idea of what I was all about.

The only trouble was, I could never convince anyone it was a picture of me and not Woody.

Then, in a Saturday night wolf-pack raid on Vassar, Woody and I found ourselves pursuing the same blonde. She preferred me. On the drive back, Flagler screamed that I was a Judas and no longer his friend.

For a month he talked around me, stared through me and refused to acknowledge I existed, which in a way, since I had become him, I didn't mind.

That winter, in one of the final journal entries, I wrote: "I have no ideas and no reason for anything. I am nothing. I couldn't even complain if somebody wanted to kill me."

Or why not step out in front of a truck?

I announced I was leaving school. I'd go south, where it was warm, and I'd write. Nobody cared. As I was waiting for a midnight cab, Mark Marshall came to my room. He understood something of rejection. "Don't go. I'll miss you," he said quietly. That scrap of affection was all I needed.

"But how do I think?" I begged.

He mentioned Occam's Razor. "Shave away the nonessentials and you'll find the real." I complained that I had already done that and I had found nothing.

On a day soon after I visited Mark, Flagler was in the room. Somebody asked Flagler, "Do you think war is always wrong?"

"That depends if you think life is sacred or not," Woody threw out.

To Pop, not only war, but any harm—even to a tree branch—was wrong.

To Pop, life *was* sacred. Sure, he never said that but he must have thought that, or felt it.

I heard Flagler's words as if they were Pop's. "Life is sacred," I heard as my silent father's motto of mottoes.

Besides, what was the value of trying to figure out life if you didn't honor life itself? I concluded.

With my new first premise, I treated others with reverence. But then I was to be revered too. Pop could have said that. I did without imitations of others. Over the years a voice emerged that I came to recognize as my own.

In the summer of 1961, I treated my summer newspaper reporter's job as a public-duty office set up for the protection of human dignity. I complained to a caption writer about his description of an overturned car and the injured people under it as AN UPSIDE DOWN WORLD. The guy roared at me that he had been writing captions for twenty years.

Closing out the journal I wrote: "Flippancy to any living thing, even an ear of corn, is wrong. Every action is moral. Every action must be excellent."

It wasn't *the* Truth from *the* God, but it was a truth I remembered from long ago, and it would do.

Pop had left me his gentleness, his caring, the possibility of something sacred.

This was all I needed to know about my hidden father.

And probably all I will ever need to know about anything.

The Chevy

AFTER college I went away to teach for a year and then left for Europe, for Rome.

Pop died politely while I was there, so that I could have time to get a plane and be at his funeral.

After the funeral, I bought Pop's '61 Chevy Biscayne sedan from Mom.

Pop had cared well for the car. He did it himself. Although it had 80,000 miles on it, the Chevy ran without burning oil and without breakdown for the next seven years.

Now and then on the Chevy's radio I'd tune in fundamentalist sermons and hymns and try to guess how it had been with Pop and me.

Pop's Chevy transported my wife and me and our

furniture to a new apartment overlooking the Hudson River.

On weekends, gangs of boys brought their beer to the riverbank and drank it in the sun. We could hear shouts and bottles breaking fourteen-floors up. One of the boys lifted the Chevy's hood and walked off with the battery. I bought a new one and chained and locked the hood.

The next Saturday night, the police told me the Chevy had been stolen, driven to the top of a hill and turned loose.

Sunday morning my wife and I climbed the hill following first a path through the woods, then a dirt road. We passed a shuttered Hudson River farmhouse. Farther up the hill, a new apartment building was rising. A big American flag flew from the top of a derrick. Signs warned that the property was protected by trained attack dogs. People had been using the area for a dump.

Then we saw the Chevy. It had crashed into a dirt bank. The impact had driven the front end into the radiator and snapped off a door. From the shredded rear tires, I knew what they had done to the transmission. The glove compartment had been pried open and maps, a spare fuel pump and the contents of a first-aid kit had been scattered on the road. A large rock held the accelerator to the floor. Three unopened bottles of beer lay in the back seat.

We removed as much camping gear as we could carry from the trunk. When came back later, the

143

stripping of the car had already begun. I chased three kids. The beer was gone.

Minutes before he died, Pop had worked on the Chevy, checking the water, oil, tires, and the tools in the trunk. The next day he was to have traveled into the Pocono Mountains and repaired industrial switchgear for GE. When I bought the Chevy, the tools in the trunk were just as Pop had arranged them the night he died.

I suppose I could have stopped the stripping of the Chevy.

I could have had it towed to a garage. I could have asked the police to watch it.

But the car was worth less than the price of repairs.

The kids snapped the hood chain and carried off the new battery. They took all they wanted from the engine. They jimmied open the trunk and stole the spare tire, tools and jack. They took the radio and two wheels and they broke all the windows with rocks.

The junk man said he never saw anything like it, kids so thoroughly destructive.